THE ARTS AND SCIENCES

A SOURCEBOOK ON COLONIAL AMERICA

THE ARTS AND SCIENCES

A SOURCEBOOK ON COLONIAL AMERICA

Edited by Carter Smith

AMERICAN ALBUMS FROM THE COLLECTIONS OF
THE LIBRARY OF CONGRESS

THE MILLBROOK PRESS, *Brookfield, Connecticut*

Cover: "The Flamingo," from Mark Catesby's The Natural History of Carolina, Florida and the Bahama Islands, *1731.*

Title Page: "A View of West Point on the Hudson River," by Pierre-Charles L'Enfant, 1782.

Contents Page: Bookplate for the New York Society Library, eighteenth century.

Back Cover: "An Indian Chief," watercolor by John White, 1587.

Library of Congress Cataloging-in-Publication Data

The Arts and sciences : a sourcebook on colonial America / edited by Carter Smith.
    p. cm. -- (American albums from the collections of the Library of Congress)
Includes bibliographical references and index.
    Summary: Describes and illustrates the arts and sciences of colonial and early Federal America through a variety of images produced at the time.
    ISBN 1-56294-037-6
    1. United States--Civilization--To 1783--Juvenile literature.
2. United States--Intellectual life--18th century--Juvenile literature.
3. United States--Civilization--To 1783--Sources--Juvenile literature.
4. United States--Intellectual life--18th century--Sources--Juvenile literature. 5. United States--Civilization--To 1783--Pictorial works--Juvenile literature. 6. United States--Intellectual life--18th century--Pictorial works--Juvenile literature. [1. United States--Civilization--To 1783--Sources.] I. Smith, C. Carter. II. Series.
E162.A667 1991
973.2--dc20   91-13936
                                                   CIP
                                                   AC

 Created in association with Media Projects Incorporated

C. Carter Smith, *Executive Editor*
Lelia Wardwell, *Managing Editor*
Charles A. Wills, *Consulting Editor*
Kimberly Horstman, *Researcher*
Lydia Link, *Designer*
Athena Angelos, *Photo Researcher*

The consultation of Bernard F. Reilly, Jr., Head Curator of the Prints and Photographs Division of the Library of Congress, is gratefully acknowledged.

Contents

NEW-YORK *Society* LIBRARY.

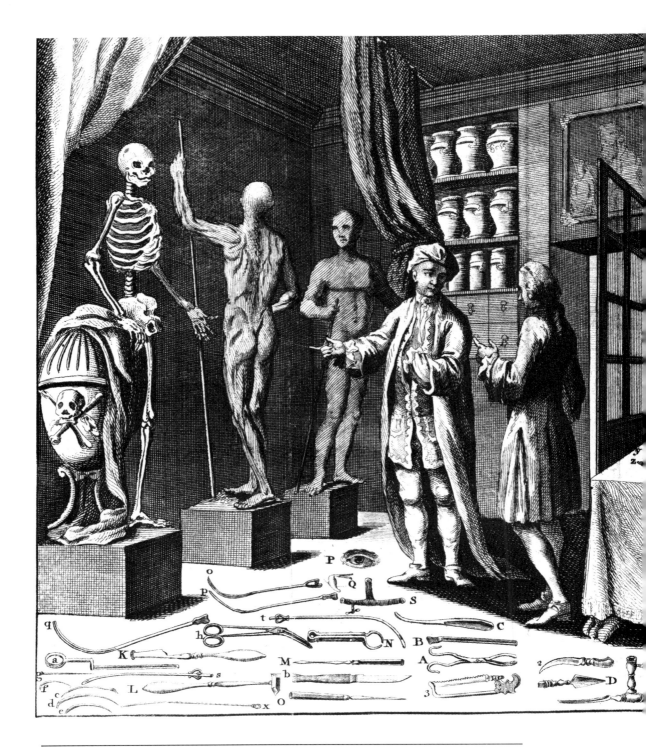

The eighteenth century saw a renewed spirit of inquiry in the arts and sciences, including medicine, in both Europe and the North American colonies. In this engraving from Universal Magazine published in London, a surgeon tutors a medical student in anatomy using a skeleton and several models of the human body. The instruments in the foreground are typical surgeon's tools of the time.

Introduction

THE ARTS AND SCIENCES is one of the initial volumes in a series published by the Millbrook Press titled AMERICAN ALBUMS FROM THE COLLECTIONS OF THE LIBRARY OF CONGRESS, and one of six books in the series subtitled SOURCEBOOKS ON COLONIAL AMERICA. They treat the early history of our homeland from its discovery and early settlement through the colonial and Revolutionary wars.

The editors' basic goal for the series is to make available to the student many of the original visual documents preserved in the Library of Congress as records of the American past. THE ARTS AND SCIENCES reproduces many of the prints, broadsides, maps, and other original works preserved in the Library's special collections divisions, and a few from its general book collections.

Featured prominently in this volume are the rich holdings of engravings, photographs, illustrated books, and architectural documentation preserved in two Library divisions: the Prints and Photographs and Rare Book and Special Collection Divisions. The nation's architectural heritage, from colonial times to the twentieth century, is extensively documented in the photographs, measured drawings, and other records of the Historic American Buildings Survey. This project has been administered since the 1930s by the Department of the Interior, in cooperation with the American Institute of Architects and the Library of Congress. These records are augmented by the Library's strong collections of original, early documents of the buildings of the United States, such as master architectural drawings and historical prints. B. Henry Latrobe's watercolor and ink rendering of his design for a theater to be built in Richmond and William Birch's view of the Chestnut Street Theatre in Philadelphia reveal much about the arts of both design and theater in America in the eighteenth century.

The progress of the other fine arts in America is represented here primarily through photographic or engraved reproductions. (The Library does not collect original paintings and sculpture.) Some engraved plates, however, such as Edward Savage's "Liberty in the Form of the Goddess of Youth," were in fact considered major works of art in their own right. American literature, on the other hand, is a particularly strong suit of the Library. In its rare book collections are many of the key movements of American letters. Shown here are early or first printings of poems by native authors like Phillis Wheatley, as well as European works, such as John Bunyan's *Pilgrim's Progress*, which had a formulative influence on American literature. The same collections also provide a good picture of the mass of new scientific information generated by European and native exploration of American forests, fields, and waters. These early illustrated books and magazines also provided an important means of dissemination for American inventors like John Fitch and Eli Whitney.

The works reproduced here represent a small but telling portion of the rich record of the cultural and scientific achievements of the colonial and early federal periods, preserved by the Library of Congress in its role as the nation's library.

BERNARD F. REILLY, JR.

A TIMELINE OF MAJOR EVENTS

1490-1599

WORLD HISTORY

Columbus departs from Spain

1492 Spain is finally united under Ferdinand and Isabella; the nation is now able to devote attention to exploration. Christopher Columbus claims the New World for Spain.

1517 German monk Martin Luther protests abuses in the Roman Catholic Church, beginning the Protestant Reformation.

1520 Ferdinand Magellan, a Portuguese explorer and navigator sailing for Spain, reaches the Pacific Ocean by sailing through the straits named after him at the foot of the South American continent. He is killed in the Philippine Islands the next year.

1534 The English Parliament passes the Act of Supremacy, acknowledging Henry VIII as head of the Church of England and beginning the English Reformation.

1559 Elizabeth I becomes Queen of England.

1569 Gerardus Mercator publishes the first cylindrical world map showing longitude, latitude, and the equator.

1588 The Spanish Armada sails from Spain hoping to invade and conquer England; the fleet is destroyed by a combination of English warships and storms.

AMERICAN HISTORY GOVERNMENT

Pope Alexander VI

1494 Pope Alexander VI issues the Treaty of Torsedillas, dividing the New World between Spain and Portugal.

1512 Spain issues the Laws of Burgos, which are designed to protect Indians from cruel treatment in Spain's colonies.

1518 Charles V, King of Spain and the Holy Roman Emperor, allows African slaves to be sent to the New World.

1532 To strengthen its colonies, the Spanish government requires ships sailing to the New World to carry livestock and seeds for crops.

1542 The Spanish government ends the practice of *encomienda*, a system that allowed colonists to either tax New World Native Americans or force them to work.

1570 Five Indian tribes in northeastern North America join together to form the Iroquois Confederacy.

Totem of the Five Nations of the Iroquois Confederacy

1583 Sir Humphrey Gilbert is granted a patent to colonize North America by Queen Elizabeth of England.

AMERICAN HISTORY ARTS AND SCIENCES

1493 Christopher Columbus's letter describing his historic voyage of discovery is published in Barcelona, Spain. Some sixteen editions are printed before 1500. An illustrated edition is published in Switzerland in 1493.

1500 A map of the New World, painted by Juan de la Casa, a pilot on Columbus's 1492 voyage, shows islands in the West Indies.

1540s Spanish missionary Bartolomé de Las Casas writes *Brevissima Relacion de las Destruction de las Indias*, a bitter condemnation of the Spanish explorers' and colonists' cruel treatment of Native American Indians.

1555 The first Aztec dictionary is published.

1564 French artist Jacques Le Moyne paints forty-two views of Indian life in Florida while accompanying the short-lived French colony there.

1566 *Discours de l'Histoire de la Floride*, an account of the unsuccessful French colony, is written by Nicholas le Challeux.

1585 John White, an English artist and explorer, paints a series of seventy-five remarkable watercolors of Indian life in the area around the ill-fated Roanoke Colony.

1588 Thomas Hariot's *A Briefe and True Account of the New Found Land of Virginia* is published in London. It is an important eyewitness account of the New World.

1590 Theodore de Bry of Holland publishes Jacques Le Moyne's

1605 Spanish author Miguel de Cervantes publishes Part I of his novel, *Don Quixote de la Mancha*.

1609 The Italian astronomer and physicist Galileo, builds a telescope.
•Johann Kepler, a German astronomer, discovers the elliptical orbit of Mars.

1611 A new English translation of the Bible, authorized by King

William Shakespeare

James, is published.

1616 Poet and playwright William Shakespeare, greatest writer of the Elizabethan era and probably in all English literature, dies

at his home in Stratford-upon-Avon.

1618 The Thirty Years' War, originally between Protestants and Catholics in central Europe, begins.

1630-42 Some 16,000 colonists from England emigrate to Massachusetts.

1637 Russian explorers reach the Pacific Ocean, having crossed Siberia.

1642 The English Civil War begins; it is a conflict between supporters of Charles I and the Church of England and the largely Puritan supporters of Parliamentary government led by Oliver Cromwell. Many supporters of the king emigrate to America.
•Montreal is founded by the French.

1643 Louis XIV, the "Sun King," begins a seventy-two-year reign as king of France.

1606 James I of England charters two companies, the Plymouth Company and the Virginia Company, to establish colonies in North America.

1607 The Jamestown Colony is founded; the settlement is governed by a council under the supervision of the Virginia Company in England.

1619 The first elected assembly in English North America—the

Virginia House of Burgesses—holds its first session at Jamestown.

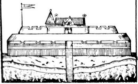

Seal of the Virginia Company

1620 The Pilgrims sign the Mayflower Compact while still aboard the *Mayflower*, binding the signers to obey "just and equal laws."

1623 "According to the commendable custom of England," the Pilgrims establish trial by twelve-man jury at Plymouth.

1635 A Maryland Indian leader protests the colony's insistence that the Indians obey English law; instead, he

suggests the colonists "conform to the customs of our country."

Fort Christina

1638 Swedish colonists found Fort Christina near what is now Wilmington, Delaware.

---

engravings about North America, as part of a series titled *Grands et Petits Voyages*.

Captain John Smith

1608 Captain John Smith's book, *A True*

Relation of Occurrences in Virginia, is published in London.

1612 John Smith's map of Virginia is published.

1613 Samuel de Champlain's *Les Voyages*, describing his explorations in Canada, is published.

1616 John Smith's *A Description of New England* appears in London.
•Pocahontas, the Indian

Pocahontas

princess who married John Rolfe of the Jamestown colony, is painted by an unknown artist while visiting London.

1624 John Smith's *Generall Historie of Virginia* is published.

1640 *The Bay Psalme Book* is published; it is the first book printed in America.

1648 Thomas Hooker's *Survey of the Summe of Church Discipline*, which summarizes the beliefs of the Congregational Church, is published.

1650-1674

WORLD HISTORY

1651 Charles II, son of Charles I, is crowned king of Scotland; after unsuccessfully invading England, he flees to France.

1652 England declares war on Holland.

1654 The Treaty of Westminster ends the first Anglo-Dutch War.

1659 The Peace of the Pyrenees ends the war between France and Spain; Spanish power gradually declines while France becomes the dominant power in Europe.

1660 The monarchy is restored in England, with Charles II as king.

1666 London is almost destroyed by the "Great Fire," which starts in a bakery.

1667 France invades the

The Great Fire of London

Spanish Netherlands.

1672 William of Orange (later William III of England) is made Captain-General of the United Provinces (the Netherlands).
•England's Royal

African Company wins exclusive right to capture African slaves for sale in the New World. The monopoly covers the African coast from Morocco to the Cape of Good Hope.

AMERICAN HISTORY GOVERNMENT

1650 England's first Navigation Act gives the nation's merchants a monopoly on trade with its colonies; the law also requires colonists to sell their products only to England and to ship them aboard English vessels.

1651 The colonies are caught up in the English Civil War. In Virginia, Governor William Berkeley is forced to surrender to a Parliamentary fleet.

1652 Massachusetts declares itself a self-governing common-wealth; New England, being mostly Puritan, supports the Parliamentary cause in England.

1653 Peter Stuyvesant allows some local government in New Amsterdam, but says his power to rule "comes from God and the company, not a few ignorant citizens."

1658 The first colonial police force is organized in New Amsterdam.

1660 Virginia passes the first of many laws defining the status of slavery and depriving slaves of legal rights; most other colonies adopt similar "slave codes." Dutch traders had brought the first slaves to Virginia in 1619.

1670 The great political philosopher John Locke writes the Fundamental Constitutions, setting up the legal framework for English settlements in the Carolinas.

John Locke

AMERICAN HISTORY ARTS AND SCIENCES

Anne Bradstreet's book of poems

1650 Anne Bradstreet of Ipswich, Massachusetts, becomes America's first published poet when her collection of poems, *The Tenth Muse*, is published in London.

1650 John Eliot, a missionary dedicated to converting Indians to Christianity, publishes a bible in the Algonquian Indian language.

1671 Two additional Indian language books, also by John Eliot, *Indian ABC* and *Indian Dialogues*, are printed.

Reverend John Eliot

1673 Judge Samuel Sewall of Salem, Massachusetts, begins a diary which will chronicle the Salem witchcraft trials over which he presided. (His diary covered the periods from 1673-1676 and 1686-1725. In 1697, he publicly confessed the court's errors in sending many accused "witches" to the gallows.)

1678 Rumors of a "Popish Plot" to restore Catholicism in England lead to anti-Catholic persecutions and laws.

1685 Louis XIV of France revokes the Edict of Nantes, renewing conflict between French Catholics and Protestants.

1686 Edmund Halley, the English astronomer who later had the famous comet named after him, publishes the

King Louis XIV

first weather chart in London.

1688 In the bloodless "Glorious Revolution," England's Catholic king James II is overthrown; he is replaced by his Protestant Dutch son-in-law, William III, who rules jointly with Queen Mary.

1689 The English Parliament passes a Declaration of Rights, limiting royal power and prohibiting Catholics from ruling.

•Peter the Great becomes czar of Russia and brings European technology to that nation.
•The War of the Grand Alliance breaks out, pitting France against the coalition of states (including England and Spain) that make up the League of Augsburg.

1697 The Treaty of Ryswick ends the War of the Grand Alliance; there is no clear winner, but France gives up some territory.

King Philip

1675 King Philip's War, between English colonists and Native American tribes in Massachusetts, Rhode

Island, and Connecticut, causes damage or destruction in sixty-four colonial towns and destroys many Indian villages.

1682 After almost two years of traveling down the Mississippi River, René Robert Cavelier, sieur de La Salle, reaches the river's mouth and claims all the land along its banks for France— a territory he names Louisiana.
•William Penn founds

Philadelphia and the Pennsylvania colony as a refuge for Quakers and other persecuted religious minorities.

1687 To assert the Crown's authority, Royal Governor Sir Edmund Andros demands Connecticut's original charter. According to some accounts, colonists hide the charter in a hollow oak tree in Hartford in order to frustrate Andros.

1696 Parliament passes another Navigation Act, setting up a board of trade to oversee commerce with the colonies.

1697 William Penn proposes a congress with representatives from all the colonies.

1699 Virginia's capital is moved from Jamestown to Williamsburg.

1683 In Philadelphia, William Bradford publishes an almanac titled *America's Messenger*.

1687 In Philadelphia, James Porteus, a trained British architect, begins building one of the earliest Georgian style structures in America. Called the Slate Roof House because of its slate roof, it became the home of William Penn in 1700.

1690 Benjamin Harris

writes the *New England Primer*.

1693 In Williamsburg, Virginia, the Reverend James Blair returns from London with master builder Thomas Hadley and the plans for the College of William and Mary—said to be drawn by Sir Christopher Wren, England's Surveyor General.
•William Bradford is appointed Royal Printer of the New York colony.

The College of William and Mary

A TIMELINE OF MAJOR EVENTS

WORLD HISTORY

1701 The question of who will rule Spain and its empire leads to the War of the Spanish Succession; eventually, Spain and France are opposed by England, Holland, and several other states.
•Frederick, ruler of Brandenburg, becomes the first king of Prussia.

1704 Forces led by England's Duke of Marlborough win a

The Duke of Marlborough

major victory over France and Spain in the Battle of Blenheim.

1713 The Treaty of Utrecht ends the War of the Spanish Succession.

1714 Queen Anne of England dies and is succeeded by the German George I, elector of Hanover and a great-grandson of James I.

1718 England declares war on Spain; France follows a year later.

1720 France's treasury is bankrupted after the Mississippi Company is

Seal of the Mississippi Company

revealed to be a sham.

1722 Dutch explorer Jacob Roggeveen discovers a remote island in the Pacific Ocean on Easter Sunday, and names it Easter Island.

AMERICAN HISTORY GOVERNMENT

1702 Delaware sets up a government separate from Pennsylvania.
•Queen Anne's War (in Europe called the War of the Spanish Succession) brings fighting in Canada between French and English colonists.

1704 The New York Assembly seizes power from the royal governor.

1712 North Carolina separates from South

Carolina and gets its own governor.

1716 Virginia governor Alexander Spotswood leads an expedition into the western most Virginia territory, crossing the Blue Ridge Mountains into the Shenandoah River valley.

1718 The French under Governor sieur de Bienville found New Orleans on the Gulf of

A French colonial cottage

Mexico at the mouth of the Mississippi River. French settlements in Louisiana flourish until 1729, when wars with several Indian tribes break out.
•Spanish settlers found

the military post and mission of San Antonio in what is now Texas.

1722 The six nations of the Iroquois Confederacy (Mohawk, Oneida, Cayuga, Seneca, and Tuscarora) sign a treaty with the Virginia colonists and agree not to cross the Potomac River or move west of the Blue Ridge Mountains.

AMERICAN HISTORY ARTS AND SCIENCES

1700 *The Selling of Joseph*, by Samuel Sewall, is the first book published in America to protest slavery.
•Henrietta Johnson, the first known female artist in America, is active as a portrait painter in Charleston, South Carolina.

1704 The first organ built in the British colonies is made in Philadelphia.

1709-1741 William Byrd writes his diaries and historical accounts of Virginia.

1712 Cotton Mather's *Thirteen Letters on Natural History and Biology* is published.

1716 The first theater in the colonies is built in Williamsburg, Virginia.

1720s The mission church of San José y

San José y San Miguel de Aguayo mission church

San Miguel de Aguayo, one of the great Spanish churches in the United States, is founded. Construction begins around 1740 and is

not completed until 1779. Referred to as the "Queen of Missions," its entrance has beautiful carvings executed by Pedro Huizar in the late eighteenth century.

1720 Inoculation for smallpox begins in Boston. A strong advocate for its use is Cotton Mather.

1724 Paul Dudley publishes a book on North American fruit trees.

Jonathan Swift

1726 Irish author Jonathan Swift's novel, *Travels into Several Remote Nations of the World*, popularly known as *Gulliver's Travels*, enjoys instant success.

1730 Russia and China sign trade agreements and a treaty of friendship.

1737 Swedish botanist Carl von Linné, also known as Linnaeus, publishes his *Genera Plantarum*, introducing an important way of classifying plants and animals.

1740 Frederick II, "the Great," becomes king of Prussia.

1742 Indian slaves in Peru, led by Juan Santos, rebel against the Spanish and defeat them in several battles.

1745 Charles Edward Stuart, "Bonnie Prince Charlie," grandson of James II, arrives in Scotland in an attempt to restore Britain to Stuart rule.
•The War of the Austrian Succession begins when Frederick II of Prussia invades Maria Teresa's Austrian province of Silesia. The Treaty of Aix-la-Chapelle ends the war and returns all lands to Austria except Silesia.

1729 French soldiers in the Louisiana Territory massacre Natchez Indians, beginning a ten-year war between the French and the Indians.

1733 James Edward Oglethorpe founds the city of Savannah and the colony of Georgia, the last of the original thirteen English colonies, as a haven for the poor.
•In New York, John Peter Zenger begins publication of the *New York Weekly Journal*. He is appointed the official printer for the colonies of New York and New Jersey after being acquitted of libel in a 1735 trial that established the principle of freedom of the press in the colonies.

1737 Jews are denied the right to vote in New York.

1744 King George's War breaks out in North America between English colonists and French colonists and their Indian allies. New Englanders capture Fort Louisbourg on Cape Breton Island but fail to take Montreal and Quebec. The war ends in 1748 with Fort Louisbourg returned to the French.

1749 Georgia permits large landholdings and slavery, leading to economic prosperity for plantation owners.

The Zenger Trial

1725 William Bradford begins publication of the *New York Gazette.*
•A portrait of Cotton Mather by Peter Pelham is the first mezzotint engraving to be made in America.
•The first botanical garden in America is opened in Philadelphia by John Bartram.
• Benjamin Franklin is twenty-four years old, and begins publication of *The Pennsylvania Gazette*. He is the editor, publisher, and printer.

1731 In Philadelphia, Benjamin Franklin founds the first subscription library.

1732 Benjamin Franklin begins publication of *Poor Richard's Almanack*.

1738 John Singleton Copley and Benjamin West, two of the best-known American painters of their era, are born.

1741 Charles Willson Peale, a distinguished artist, naturalist, and inventor, is born.

1747 Benjamin Franklin's pamphlet, *Plain Truth*, is published in Philadelphia. It contains a political cartoon titled "The Waggoner and Hercules," said to be the first to appear in British North America.

1748 The Ephrata Press publishes *Der Blutige Schau-Platz*, a history of German Protestant martyrs.

A TIMELINE OF MAJOR EVENTS

1750·1774

WORLD HISTORY

Frederick the Great

1750 Famed composer Johann Sebastian Bach dies in Germany.

1756 Frederick the Great learns of a secret agreement between six European states (including France and Russia) to divide up Prussia between them; the Seven Years' War begins with a Prussian attack on Austria. Britain allies itself with Prussia and declares war on France.
•William Pitt the Elder becomes Britain's secretary of state; his vigorous leadership plays a major role in Britain's rise as a world power.

1757 Robert Clive establishes the rule of the British East India Company over most of India.

1762 Britain gains Spanish colonies in the Caribbean and the Philippines.
•France cedes all of its territory west of the Mississippi to Spain.
•Jean-Jacques Rousseau publishes *The Social Contract*, a key text in the philosophical movement called the Enlightenment.

1763 The Treaty of Paris ends the Seven Years' War.

Jean-Jacques Rousseau

1772 In Paris, the final volumes of the French *Encyclopédie* are published. Its editor is Denis Diderot.

AMERICAN HISTORY GOVERNMENT

1753 The Liberty Bell is first rung to call a meeting of the Pennsylvania Assembly; the bell (which cracked during a testing) bears a verse from the Bible: "Proclaim Liberty throughout all the land unto all the inhabitants thereof."

1754 In Albany, New York, Benjamin Franklin proposes that the colonies and the Iroquois Confederacy unite for defense against the French and their Indian allies. The plan is rejected by the colonial legislatures.

A cartoon urging unity

1754 Competing British and French claims to territory from the Appalachians west to the Mississippi lead to nine years of fighting known as the French and Indian War.

1755 Britain banishes defeated French colonists from Acadia, some of whom travel south to Louisiana, where they become known as Acadians (Cajuns).

1760 The English capture Montreal from the French, essentially ending the war in America.

1773 Parliament passes the Tea Act, giving British merchants a monopoly on the sale of tea to the colonies. In the best-known protest against the Tea Act, Boston Patriots dump tons of tea into the city harbor; similar actions and protests take place across the colonies.

AMERICAN HISTORY ARTS AND SCIENCES

1751 Lewis Hallam establishes a theatrical repertory company in Williamsburg, Virginia.

1756 Isaiah Thomas, age six, becomes an indentured apprentice to Boston printer Zechariah Fowle. Thomas is a skilled printer who later becomes established as one of America's publishing giants.

1757 *The American*

Magazine and Monthly Chronicle is the first significant magazine to be published in the colonies.

1766 Major Robert Rogers writes *Ponteach, or the Savages of America*, a play about Pontiac's War.

1767 Thomas Godfrey's *Prince of Parthis* is the first American play staged by paid performers.

1770 Isaiah Thomas begins publication of the *Massachusetts Spy*, which competes with four other Boston newspapers: the *Evening-Post*, the *Post Boy*, the *Newsletter*, and the *Gazette*.

1771 Benjamin West paints "The Death of Wolfe."
•*Poems on Various Subjects*, by Phillis Wheatley, a young black poet from Boston, is published in London.

A book by Isaiah Thomas

1772 Charles Willson Peale paints the first life-size portrait of George Washington.

1775 Scottish inventor Isaac Watt develops an improved steam engine. He sells his first engine to the British industrialist John Wilkinson.

1776 Spain unifies its South American empire by creating the Viceroyalty of Rio de la Plata. It includes Argentina, Bolivia, Paraguay, and Uruguay.

1777 French chemist Antoine Lavoisier proves that air consists mainly

Antoine de Lavoisier

of oxygen and nitrogen.

1778 Captain James Cook discovers the Sandwich Islands, later known as Hawaii.

1781 Russia begins

construction of the Siberian highway.

1783 In France, the Montgolfier brothers build the first hot air balloon. Their flight lasts ten minutes.

1784 Russia establishes a small settlement on Kodiak Island, Alaska.

1789 In Paris, the French Revolution erupts when a mob captures the Bastille, a fortress prison.

Storming the Bastille

1776 Delegates from twelve of the thirteen colonies meet in Philadelphia. They issue the Declaration of Independence.

1777 Congress authorizes a United States flag, with thirteen stars and stripes.

1778 The Continental Congress approves the Articles of Confederation.

1783 The Treaty of Paris, signed by the United

States and Britain, ends the Revolutionary War.

1784 James Madison publishes *Remonstrances Against Religious Assessments*, a pamphlet that argues for the separation of church and state.

1785 Congress passes the Basic Land Ordinance. It establishes the township, an area six miles square, as the basic unit by which new territories are surveyed.

John Adams

1787 The United States Constitution goes into

effect when nine of the thirteen states ratify it.

1789 George Washington is inaugurated as the first President of the United States.

1791 Ten amendments to the Constitution are adopted. They are known as the Bill of Rights.

1797 John Adams is inaugurated as the second president of the United States.

1775 Edward Barnes writes "Yankee Doodle," to the music of an old English tune.

1776 An American engineer, David Bushnell, invents the first submarine, dubbed "Bushnell's Connecticut Turtle." The one-man vessel is unsuccessful in an attack on British ships in New York harbor.
•Thomas Paine writes *Common Sense*.

1780 The American

Academy of Arts and Sciences is founded in Boston.

1787 The first American comedy, Royall Tyler's *Contrast*, is staged.

Fitch's steamboat

1789 John Fitch demonstrates his steamboat at Philadelphia.
•President George Washington appoints Major Pierre Charles L'Enfant, a French artist, designer, and architect, to design the plan for the nation's new capital in what is today Washington, D.C.

1792 American-born painter Benjamin West is made president of London's prestigious Royal Academy.

1793 The cotton gin, which revolutionizes Southern agriculture, is invented by Eli Whitney.
•Construction of the Capitol building, designed by William Thornton, begins.

1799 *The Encyclopedia, or a Dictionary of Arts, Sciences, and Miscellaneous Literature* is published by Thomas Dobson in Philadelphia.

Part I
Colonial Arts and Architecture

This portrait of Benjamin Franklin was painted in 1785 by Charles Willson Peale (1741–1827), in his day the leading portrait painter in Pennsylvania and surrounding colonies. The portrait was one of some 250 portraits of famous men that Peale and members of his family painted for the portrait gallery of the Philadelphia Museum, one of the first public museums in the country.

The task of settling a new continent and building a nation meant that early America had a decidedly practical nature. The arts that flourished in early America shared this practical slant. Portraits, not landscapes or sweeping historical scenes, dominated the canvases. Large public sculpture was rare, but shop signs, weather vanes, gravestones, and other functional items were carefully and often beautifully carved. Architecture began simply and practically; buildings were usually made of wood, which was plentiful.

By the end of the eighteenth century, a distinctive American style had emerged. The earliest American styles in art and architecture were shaped by the limited training of American artists and architects; a simplicity and straightforwardness characterized much of the colonial period. But the Revolution brought great change to American art. The American emphasis on equality and liberty was reflected in the style of the nation's architecture and painting. Aristocratic flourishes found little favor, but the signs of prosperity and success were evident, whether in public buildings and churches, or in portraits of merchants and politicians.

The greatest influence on all types of American art was from England, although Dutch, Swedish, German, and other European settlers brought the flavor of those countries as well. Americans followed English styles through imported books and magazines, and many American arists traveled to England and the Continent to finish their education. Those who returned invariably brought the most fashionable styles back with them. American artists, particularly painters, also traveled to England and Europe and settled there. Eventually their American style, in turn, began to influence England and Europe.

NATIVE AMERICAN ART

The artistic traditions of the Native Americans were developed over thousands of years with no contact at all with the western world. The Indians created art in many different forms—sculpture, sand painting, carving, weaving, pottery—and in most cases, the designs had a religious significance. Although every tribe and region had its own traditions, Indians rarely created art for the sake of beauty alone. Animal spirits were often represented on such objects as weapons and hunting tools. Elaborate and finely-crafted designs on everyday objects were ways the tribe would honor the deities in their religion. All aspects of Indian culture, including their art and religion, were greatly affected by contact with the European settlers in the colonial period.

The Cincinnati Tablet (above) is a carved stone that was made by an American Indian. Although no one knows its actual use, some scholars think it may have been a very early printing stone used to decorate the Indians' animal-skin clothing.

This Indian rock painting (opposite, top) was drawn by Chickamauga Indians long before Europeans came to the New World. Animals and animal spirits appear more frequently than humans in ancient Indian art. This face might be a bear, or perhaps a raccoon.

These diagrams are Indian hieroglyphics, or picture writing (opposite, bottom). The Indians had no alphabet and no written language, but they used pictures like these to tell stories. In this scene, a warrior tells what happened during an expedition. The four stick figures are enemy warriors. The one without a head died during the battle, and the one with a skirt is a woman. They carry the weapons they used in the battle: a gun, on the left; an ax, on the right; and a bow and arrow, in the hands of the warrior who died. After the battle, the victorious warrior traveled by canoe (below the figures) with nine companions (there are nine paddles) to a meeting (the campfire) with the heads of the Bear tribe (the animal to the left of the fire) and the Turtle tribe (to the right).

THE EARLIEST COLONIAL PAINTINGS

Portraits were the only way of recording what a person looked like in early America. Colonists wanted records of themselves just as we do, perhaps to send to faraway family members, or maybe just to preserve themselves for history. Portrait painters sprang up throughout the colonies to fill the demand. Most early portrait painters were not specialists but silversmiths, sign makers, furniture makers, and other craftspeople who painted portraits on the side.

These amateur painters rarely saw the work of other artists since travel was very difficult in early America. Their lack of training and exposure to other artists produced paintings in many different styles, but they did have some things in common. For example, many of these early American artists produced work that is oddly flat, or two-dimensional, a style sometimes described as "primitive."

This engraving of Peter Stuyvesant (above) was copied from a painting by an unknown artist, who probably painted it in the 1660s. In 1647, Stuyvesant became the Director General of the Dutch West India Company, which ran the colony of New Netherland. In 1664, the colony was conquered by the English, who gave it, and the city of New Amsterdam, a new name: New York. Stuyvesant was a harsh and intolerant leader as the grim scowl in this picture suggests.

Tishcohan (left), or "He Who Never Blackens Himself," was chief of the Delaware tribe. Tishcohan posed for Gustavus Hesselius (1682–1755), one of America's leading portrait painters, in about 1735. The painting was commissioned as a historical record by John Penn, who at the time was negotiating to buy land from the Delaware tribe. The eventual agreement gave Penn all the land "a day's walk" (usually about twenty miles) from a certain tree. But Penn hired runners to run for a day, tricking the Delawares out of their land. In this portrait, considered one of Hesselius's best, Tishcohan has not yet been tricked, but a certain quiet sadness is clear in the Indian's face.

This woodcut of the Reverend Richard Mather (left), the first engraved portrait ever made in the American colonies, was taken from an oil painting. It was probably created by John Foster (1648–81), a printer and publisher in Boston. Foster's trade led him naturally into engraving, since the books he printed often needed illustrations.

This Pennsylvania German colonist (right) has an appropriately bright and cheery air, for he decorates a kind of wooden box—sometimes called a "gift" or "bride" box—that probably held festive or ceremonial clothing. Decorations like this one on everyday items such as boxes and furniture were very popular in early colonial times.

BENJAMIN WEST

Benjamin West was born in rural Pennsylvania. He showed an interest in drawing at an early age; by eight he was considered an artistic genius. He began painting portraits for money as a teenager. At eighteen, West left the countryside and moved to Philadelphia, and not long afterward to New York. Then, in 1759, at the age of twenty-one, he left New York for Italy, never to return. He eventually settled permanently in London, and soon became one of King George III's favorite painters. In 1792, West became president of England's Royal Academy.

West painted mostly portraits during his years in America, like other colonial painters. But in Europe he began to make large, sweeping paintings of historical and religious subjects. This style, called "neoclassical," was borrowed from the art of ancient Greece and Rome.

American artists of the day often traveled to Europe to refine their painting skills, and they usually found their way to West's studio in London. Several of America's most famous painters, including Gilbert Stuart and John Singleton Copley, were among his students. Although West was still young when he left America, he is an important figure in American art. He was the first American-born painter to win fame in Europe, and he inspired a whole generation of American artists. His work also influenced the next generation of English artists.

William Penn (above), was the founder of Pennsylvania. The engraving is taken from Benjamin West's 1772 historical painting, "William Penn's Treaty with the Indians." West made the painting for Penn's son, Thomas.

Matthew Pratt (1734-1805) painted this portrait (right) of Benjamin West's wife between 1764 and 1766, when he was working in West's London studio. West used his considerable influence in the art world to help the careers of younger American painters such as Pratt who would remember him as both a teacher and a friend.

GILBERT STUART

Gilbert Stuart (1755–1828) was probably the most famous portrait painter of the early American period. Stuart was born in Rhode Island in 1755 and began to study art as a teenager. He studied in Scotland for several years, returned to Rhode Island briefly, and then moved to London in 1775. There he studied under Benjamin West and quickly became a very popular portrait painter. In 1787, Stuart moved from London to Ireland and stayed there for five years. Then he returned permanently to America, painting first in Philadelphia, then in Washington, and finally in Boston, where he settled in 1805.

Stuart's reputation as a brilliant portrait painter rests on his ability to show the character of his subjects. He was more interested in painting faces than in painting the rich clothing and settings that most people demanded in their portraits. Indeed, several of his most famous paintings are unfinished, showing only the faces of his subjects, but those faces are so powerful that the rest of the painting seems almost unnecessary.

Gilbert Stuart's portrait of Don Josef de Jaudenes y Nebot (above, top), a Spanish diplomat, was painted in New York in the late eighteenth century. Stuart's beautiful rendition of the Spaniard's elaborate clothing combines with the diplomat's slightly haughty face to portray his aristocratic arrogance.

Stuart painted this portrait of James Greenleaf (above, bottom), a successful American businessman, in 1795. Stuart also painted a second, slightly less fancy portrait of Greenleaf around the same time, but this is considered the more beautiful of the two.

This portrait of George Washington, known as the Lansdowne portrait, was painted in Philadelphia in 1796. The full-length, formal pose was one Stuart usually avoided, and although this is now one of the most famous paintings of Washington, the artist considered it a failure. Stuart actually made three paintings like this one. The original was for Philadelphia businessman William Bingham, who was so pleased with it that he ordered a copy to give to his English friend, Lord Lansdowne. Because an engraving of Lansdowne's copy was the first to be widely distributed, his version was considered the "original" painting.

JOHN SINGLETON COPLEY

John Singleton Copley (1738–1815) is usually considered the greatest early American painter. Copley was born in Boston and by the age of nineteen had become a successful portrait painter in that city. When he was in his late twenties, he sent a painting to London to be exhibited. It was a great success, and artists there began urging Copley to come to England.

Copley's greatest ambition was to paint historical subjects—the most noble and worthy sort of painting, according to the art world of the time. But Americans were busy building a nation, and few were interested in historical painting. Meanwhile, Copley was earning a very good living painting portraits and he decided to stay in America.

In 1774, however, as war between England and the colonies began to seem likely, Copley left America to settle in London. There he began to paint historical scenes, and developed a more sophisticated European style. Most modern critics, however, prefer the simplicity of Copley's American portraits and consider them to be his finest work.

This painting of Samuel Adams, one of Copley's most famous portraits, was done in America in the early 1770s. It shows Adams confronting Thomas Hutchinson, the governor of Massachusetts, after the Boston Massacre of March 1770. Adams is pointing to the royal charter for the colony with one hand and holding a statement of protest from the citizens of Boston in the other. Copley's dark, quiet background contrasts with Adams's highlighted face and hands to create a masterful portrayal of this famous politician's angry dignity.

Copley met Mr. and Mrs. Ralph Izard in Naples in 1775 and painted this portrait of them shortly afterward. The painter traveled extensively in Italy before settling in London, and this large double portrait is one of the first paintings to reflect his new familiarity with ancient Greek and Roman art. An ancient vase stands above Mr. Izard's head, a classical marble sculpture fills the center of the painting, and the Roman Coliseum can be seen in the background.

JOHN TRUMBULL

John Trumbull (1756–1843) was born in Connecticut, where his father was governor. He was the first American painter to come from an upper-class rather than a crafts background, and he decided to become a painter, despite his family's disapproval, after meeting John Singleton Copley in 1773.

During the Revolutionary War, Trumbull served as an aide to General George Washington, who valued his map-drawing skills. He was known as Colonel Trumbull for the rest of his life, although he resigned from the army in 1777.

In 1780, Trumbull traveled to London to study painting, and like many other young American painters there, he became a student of Benjamin West's. Trumbull decided to concentrate on historical painting, which he felt was the most worthy kind, and in 1785 began the first of a long series of paintings commemorating the people and events of the American Revolution.

Trumbull moved back and forth between England and America several times, and abandoned his career in painting more than once for unsuccessful business ventures. He eventually settled in New York, where he became a successful portrait painter. The highlight of his career, however, came in 1817, when he won a commission from the United States Congress to paint four enormous historical paintings for the rotunda of the Capitol. His twelve-by-eighteen-foot paintings depicting the birth of the nation are still displayed there today.

This engraving of John Trumbull was done by Asher Brown Durand, who became well-known after engraving Trumbull's famous painting of the signing of the Declaration of Independence. The original portrait of Trumbull was painted by Samuel L. Waldo and William Jewett, who ran an important New York portrait-painting company from about 1820 to 1854.

This Trumbull portrait of Alexander Hamilton was painted from other likenesses after Hamilton's death in 1804. Trumbull's model for this, and several others like it, was a marble bust of Hamilton made by the Italian sculptor Giuseppe Ceracchi. The portrait, like its marble model, is stiff and formal.

This engraving of a pencil sketch by Trumbull shows a Creek Indian. Trumbull traveled widely to collect accurate portraits of famous men—as well as unknown ones, such as this Indian—for his historical paintings. His pencil sketches, done from life, were often delicate and subtle, and were sometimes better than the finished portraits based on them.

PAINTERS AND AMERICAN HISTORY

Most colonial painters followed the European trend in considering historical themes the most worthy and elevated subjects for a painter, but historical painting did not become popular until after the Revolutionary War, when Americans saw that their own deeds had made history and were worthy of commemoration. John Trumbull was the best-known early American painter of historical scenes, in part because he had very little competition. Other American artists, including Benjamin West and John Singleton Copley, did not become major historical painters until they moved to England. They also tended to paint scenes from the more distant past.

One reason for painting scenes from recent history, like the Revolution, was to preserve an accurate visual record of them. When John Trumbull went to Congress to ask for a commission to paint the four large murals that decorate the Capitol today, he argued that no other painter had seen, and painted from life, so many of the major figures that took part in the events.

This engraving of the Battle of Lexington (opposite, top) was made in 1798 by Cornelius Tiebout, one of the earliest American-born engravers. Tiebout first learned to engrave from a colonial silversmith, but he traveled to England in 1793 to improve his skills under James Heath, a famous English engraver.

Trumbull's "Death of General Montgomery in the Attack on Quebec" (opposite, bottom) was one of the painter's earliest, and most artistically successful, historical paintings. It was finished in 1786, the second painting in a series about the Revolutionary War that Trumbull began while he was studying in London. Trumbull greatly admired Montgomery's bold attack on Quebec during a blizzard in December 1775.

In this engraving of a painting by Benjamin West (below), British colonel Henry Bouquet is holding a peace conference with a group of Indians from the Ohio River valley. This meeting took place in October 1764, a year after the conclusion of the French and Indian War. Although the British were the victors in this conflict, tensions remained between the British and the Indians on the western frontier.

Trumbull's "Resignation of General Washington" (opposite, top) was the last of the four large paintings made for the rotunda of the Capitol. Trumbull considered Washington's resignation at the end of the Revolutionary War "one of the highest moral lessons ever given to the world," since unlike most famous leaders before him, Washington voluntarily surrendered his power after leading the Continental Army to victory.

This unfinished painting by Benjamin West (opposite, bottom) is called "The Signing of the Preliminary Treaty of Peace." West began the painting in 1783, a year after the initial peace treaty between America and Britain was signed in Paris. It shows five American diplomats— including Benjamin Franklin, John Jay, and John Adams— but was left unfinished because West was never able to get the British diplomats to pose for him.

Trumbull made two paintings of the Surrender of Lord Cornwallis at Yorktown. The first was part of the series of Revolutionary War paintings he began in London; the second (below) was for the rotunda of the Capitol. Despite the painting's title it wasn't Cornwallis who actually surrendered. The British commander-in-chief claimed to be sick and sent his assistant, General Charles O'Hara. Washington responded by sending General Benjamin Lincoln (on the horse) to accept the British surrender. Trumbull made every effort to paint a historically accurate picture. He traveled to Paris to paint the portraits of the French figures and to Yorktown to sketch the scene. But he did make one obvious mistake: His American flag has thirteen stars but fourteen stripes.

COPLEY'S "WATSON AND THE SHARK"

John Singleton Copley's "Watson and the Shark," completed in London in 1778, was the artist's first great historical painting. The shark attack on the fourteen-year-old Brook Watson took place in the harbor of the Cuban city of Havana in 1749. Brook Watson survived the attack (although he lost a leg) and went on to become a successful London businessman. Watson may even have commissioned the painting from Copley, although this isn't certain.

The painting shows the terrifying moment just before the rescue was completed: Watson has been bitten; one seaman is ready to spear the shark and another has thrown Watson a rope, but the boy's life is still in danger. It is interesting to note that the black rescuer is one of the first artistic representations of a black man in a flattering role. By addressing a true and terrifying but historically unimportant event, Copley heralded a new period in painting: Romanticism. The Romantics celebrated the emotions of ordinary life, not just those of heroes at great moments in history.

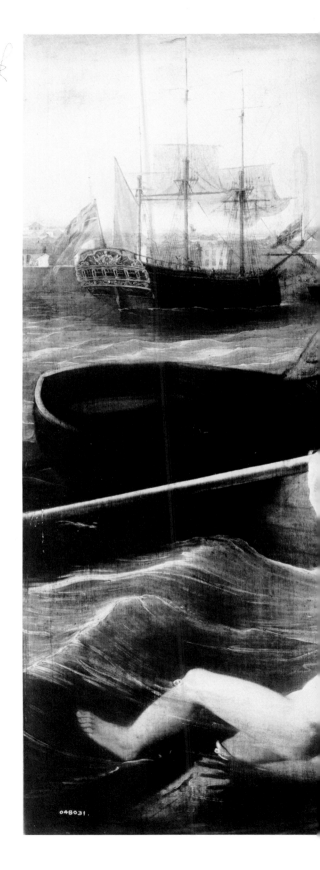

048031.

PAINTING THE AMERICAN LANDSCAPE

Because the majority of early American paintings are portraits, scholars believed for many years that portraits were almost the only kind of painting made during America's early years. They now believe that although landscapes were always much rarer than portraits, many landscape paintings simply didn't survive–partly because few colonial settlers considered the untamed land of America beautiful. They were accustomed to the neat fields and gardens of Europe. Slowly, however, the settlers began to see beauty in the wild scenery of their new homes, and artists began to commemorate it.

"View from the Green Woods Towards Canaan and Salisbury in Connecticut" (opposite, top), an etching attributed to Trenchard, appeared in the Columbian Magazine *in 1789.*

This engraving of "A Distant View of the Falls of Niagara" (opposite, bottom) is an illustration from a history of the American Revolution published in London in about 1788.

This etching (below), called "View of a Pass over South Mountain from York Town to Carlisle," depicts a road in Pennsylvania. It was published as the frontispiece of the May 1788 issue of the Columbian Magazine. *The* Columbian, *founded in 1786, was one of the highest quality magazines of the era. In addition to interesting and varied articles and essays, it published a wide variety of engravings. The artist was probably Thomas Bedwell (1779–95), a Philadelphia engraver and miniature painter.*

CITY VIEWS AND DAILY LIFE

In addition to scenes of rural beauty, early American artists painted many views of the cities and towns of their day. They often chose to illustrate these cities at some important moment in history. For example, a famous naval battle offered the chance to paint a city as well as its harbor and the many ships involved. But artists also painted many everyday scenes, and such pictures offer us an important glimpse into American life. Like rural scenes, early American city landscapes almost always included human figures, which helped to set the scale and add interest to the paintings.

Charles Willson Peale made this etching (right) of a street scene in Philadelphia in 1787. It is the earliest known etching by an American painter. Entitled "Accident on Lombard Street," the illustration includes a caption that reads: "The pye from Bake-house she had brought / But let it fall for want of thought / And laughing sweeps collect around / The pye that's scatter'd on the ground."

This view of Boston in 1777 (below) was engraved by François Haberman. The cannon in the middle of the street is evidence of the Revolutionary War, which had begun two years earlier.

RELIGIOUS AND PATRIOTIC SUBJECTS

Interest in religious and patriotic paintings developed late in America. In New England, the Puritans rejected the worldly artistic tradition of European Catholicism. They permitted portraits, but they forbade the painting of religious subjects. The Anglican Church, which was established in many of the southern colonies, did not forbid religious paintings, but when they were needed they were usually imported from Europe. Gustavus Hesselius, a Swedish artist who settled in America in 1712 and worked primarily in Pennsylvania and Maryland, is the only early American painter known to have painted religious scenes.

Early patriotic paintings were allegorical. That is, they used symbols, such as an eagle, to stand for abstract ideas, like liberty. The symbols had to be interpreted to understand the story that a painter was trying to tell. Allegorical artists often used figures from mythology in their paintings, since many gods and goddesses were closely identified with abstract ideas, such as love or war. Like historical paintings, allegories became more popular after the Revolutionary War, when Americans were eager to celebrate their victory. Liberty was an especially popular theme.

Benjamin West's "Venus Lamenting the Death of Adonis" (above) was painted in 1803. In it, Venus, the Roman goddess of love, mourns the death of Adonis, a beautiful young man whom she loved greatly. Venus's son Cupid mourns with her, one small hand draped across Adonis's neck.

"Liberty as Youth" (opposite) was painted, engraved, and published by Edward Savage in 1796. In it, a young woman (Liberty) offers support to a bald eagle, a symbol of the young United States of America, the land of liberty.

RELIGIOUS SCULPTURE IN WOOD AND STONE

Little of what we ordinarily think of as sculpture was created in America until after 1800. Unlike portraits or landscapes of American people and places, large, free-standing sculptures were rarely wanted. If they were, they could be imported from Europe. Instead, like the American Indians, early Americans put most of their sculptural energy into carving and decorating ordinary items. Furniture, kitchen tools, shop signs, and other necessities were often skillfully and beautifully decorated.

Like early American painters, early sculptors often combined one or more trades. In a small settlement, for instance, the blacksmith might be called upon to carve a shop sign. But under the difficult and dangerous conditions of colonial life, there was one area where sculpture was always in demand: the making of gravestones.

This gravestone (opposite, top) illustrates the Puritan preoccupation with life after death. Death is shown struggling with an angel, who prevents him from extinguishing the flame that symbolizes the life of the spirit.

This detail from the gravestone of Joseph Renalls (opposite, bottom), who died in New England in 1729, is a beautiful example of gravestone art. The winged face at the top symbolizes the soul rising to heaven. The inscription reads, "Serve God in Truth while in your youth & till your life doth end."

This wooden carving of the crucifixion of St. Acacius (below) is Spanish. It was found in New Mexico in the eighteenth century and is one kind of religious carvings known as "Santos figurines," or bultos.

PORTRAIT SCULPTURE

The earliest portrait sculptures in America were simple carvings of faces on gravestones. Paintings were a much more common way to preserve a person's image than sculptures, and few American sculptors possessed the skill or training to depict faces or figures well. Those who did were generally either immigrants from Europe or Americans who had traveled to Europe for training. Much of the eighteenth-century portrait sculpture of Americans was done by European artists.

This full-figure portrait of George Washington, by Jean-Antoine Houdon, is dated 1788. The state of Virginia commissioned the sculpture from Houdon, who traveled to America and stayed with Washington at Mount Vernon in 1785. The statue was placed in Virginia's capitol in 1796. Washington's formal pose and clothing are typical of the style then fashionable.

This marble bust of John Paul Jones (right) was made by the French sculptor Jean-Antoine Houdon (1741-1828). Houdon was one of the most famous sculptors of the eighteenth century and was particularly skilled in portraiture.

In this woodcut by Alexander Anderson (below), angry New Yorkers tear down a statue of King George III after hearing a reading of the Declaration of Independence on July 9, 1776 (just four days after it was adopted). The New Yorkers melted down the statue and made it into bullets for the Revolutionary War. The statue was the work of the English sculptor Joseph Wilton, and had been placed on New York's Bowling Green in 1770. It was one of the very few examples of monumental sculpture to be seen in colonial America.

THE LITERATURE OF COLONIAL AMERICA

The first book published in America was the *Whole Booke of Psalmes*, better known as the Bay Psalm Book. It was published in Cambridge, Massachusetts, in 1640. The topic of this first American book is fitting, for religious books, together with historical ones, were the most popular kinds of literature in early America.

Most of the books the early settlers read were brought with them from England and Europe. But the American printing and publishing industry, centered in Boston and Philadelphia, developed steadily after the establishment of the first printing press in Cambridge in 1639.

It was some time, however, before early American presses printed what could be called literature. Early settlers needed to tame their new land, and after religion and history, scientific and technological subjects dominated early American publishing. Newspapers were popular, and so were almanacs. Benjamin Franklin began publishing his *Poor Richard's Almanack* in 1732 and published it annually until 1757. It was full of information and advice from "Poor Richard."

By the late 1700s, plays, poetry, and even novels were becoming more popular in America. The value the early Americans placed on books and learning can be seen in the number of schools and libraries they established.

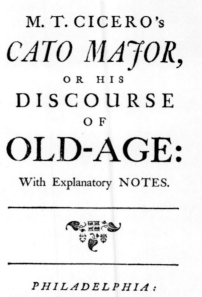

M. T. CICERO's CATO MAJOR, OR HIS DISCOURSE OF OLD-AGE: With Explanatory NOTES.

PHILADELPHIA: Printed and Sold by B. FRANKLIN, MDCCXLIV.

In 1744, Benjamin Franklin published Marcus Tullius Cicero's Cato Major *(above), the first translation of a classical work to be printed in America. In this book, Cicero, one of the greatest Roman writers, presents a dialogue in which the eighty-four-year-old Cato explains to two young friends the best way to deal with old age. Cato's statement of belief in the immortality of the soul made this work, written almost fifty years before the birth of Christ, an influence on the early Christian church.*

232.

Der Blutige Schau-Plaß, oder Martyrer Spiegel der Tauffs-Gesinnten, oder Wehrlosen Christen,

Welche in dem neunten Jahr-Hundert gelitten haben, von dem Jahr 800. (nach der Geburt Christi) an bis zu dem Jahr 900.

Kurzer Inhalt von den Martyrern dieses neunten Jahr-Hunderts.

THE
Pilgrim's Progress.
FROM
THIS WORLD TO
That which is to come.
The Second Part.
Delivered under the Similitude of a
DREAM,
Wherein is set forth
The manner of the setting out of *Christian*'s Wife and Children, their
Dangerous JOURNEY,
AND
Safe Arrival at the Desired Country.

By *JOHN BUNYAN*,

I have used Similitudes, Hof. 12. 10.

LONDON,
Printed for *Nathaniel Ponder* at the *Peacock*,
in the *Poultry*, near the Church, 1684.

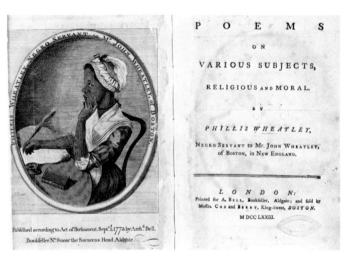

P O E M S
ON
VARIOUS SUBJECTS,
RELIGIOUS AND MORAL.

BY

PHILLIS WHEATLEY,

NEGRO SERVANT to Mr. JOHN WHEATLEY,
of BOSTON, in NEW ENGLAND.

LONDON:
Printed for A. BELL, Bookseller, Aldgate; and sold by
Messrs. COX and BERRY, King-Street, BOSTON.

MDCCLXXIII.

In 1748, the Ephrata Brotherhood, a German Baptist press in Ephrata, Pennsylvania, published The Bloody Arena *(above), a history of Mennonites who had died for their religion. The Mennonites, a German-speaking sect that began in Switzerland, sought refuge in America from religious persecution, as so many religious minorities had done. The first Mennonites arrived in 1683 and settled in Germantown, Pennsylvania.*

John Bunyan's The Pilgrim's Progress from this World to that Which Is to Come *(above, right), published in England in 1678, was one of the most influential books of its time. Bunyan wrote in a simple but beautiful style that was heavily influenced by the Bible. The Pilgrim's Progress is an allegory; it tells the story of the pilgrimage by Christian, and later his wife Christiana, from the City of Destruction to the Celestial City, or the world "that is to come."*

Phillis Wheatley's first and only book, Poems on Various Subjects, Religious and Moral *(above), was published in London in 1773, the year she was freed from slavery. Wheatley (1753–84) was born in the West African country of Senegal, where she was kidnapped by a slave trader. She was owned by John Wheatley, a Bostonian, and worked for his family (from whom she acquired her name) as a personal servant. John Wheatley allowed Phillis to be educated, which was very unusual for someone who was not only a slave but also a woman. Of the fewer than fifty poems by Wheatley that survive, eighteen are elegies—poems that express sadness or loss.*

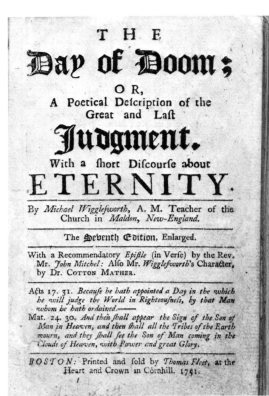

THE

Day of Doom;

OR,

A Poetical Defcription of the
Great and Laft

Judgment.

With a fhort Difcourfe about

ETERNITY.

By *Michael Wigglefworth*, A. M. Teacher of the
Church in *Maldon, New-England*.

The **Seventh Edition**, Enlarged.

With a Recommendatory *Epiftle* (in Verfe) by the Rev.
Mr. *John Mitchel*: Alfo Mr. *Wigglefworth's* Character,
by Dr. Cotton Mather.

Acts 17. 31. *Becaufe he hath appointed a Day in the which
he will judge the World in Righteoufnefs, by that Man
whom he hath ordained.*

Mat. 24. 30. *And then fhall appear the Sign of the Son of
Man in Heaven, and then fhall all the Tribes of the Earth
mourn, and they fhall fee the Son of Man coming in the
Clouds of Heaven, with Power and great Glory.*

BOSTON: Printed and fold by *Thomas Fleet*, at the
Heart and Crown in Cornhill. 1751.

THE

JOURNALS

OF

MADAM KNIGHT,

AND

REV. MR. BUCKINGHAM.

FROM THE

Original Manuscripts,

WRITTEN IN 1704 & 1710.

NEW-YORK: WILDER & CAMPBELL.

1825.

The Day of Doom *(this page, top, left) was
written by Michael Wigglesworth in 1662.
Wigglesworth (c. 1631–1705) was an
American clergyman and poet who emigrated to Massachusetts with his family in
1638.* The Day of Doom, *a religious ballad,
contained vivid images from the Bible and
was tremendously popular in New England.*

*Sarah Kemble Knight (c. 1666–1727; this
page, bottom, left), known as Madam
Knight, headed a writing school in Boston.
Her most famous book,* Private Journal of a
Journey from Boston to New York in the
Year 1704, *is a valuable source of informa-
tion on colonial customs and living condi-
tions.*

Elegiac Sonnets and Other Poems *(opposite, top), by Charlotte Smith, was published
in America in 1795 by Isaiah Thomas.
Thomas was one of the most important
publishers in early America. He founded a
newspaper called the* Massachusetts Spy.
The Spy's *support for the Revolutionary
cause brought Thomas into frequent conflict
with the British government. After the
Revolutionary War, Thomas began publishing books. Altogether he published more
than four hundred books, including the first
Bible printed in the United States.*

The Tenth Muse Lately Sprung Up in
America *(opposite, bottom left) was the first
book of poems published by Anne
Bradstreet (c. 1612–72), who is considered
one of the first significant woman authors in
America. Bradstreet arrived in Massachusetts Bay with the Puritans in 1630 and
published these poems twenty years later.*

America—a Prophesy *(opposite, bottom
right), by the Englishman William Blake
(1757-1827), was published in 1793. The
narrative is a long poem which uses facts
woven into an imaginary cloth to tell the
story of the American Revolution. It ends
with a prophecy that the American ideal—
life, liberty, and the pursuit of happiness—
would spread throughout the world. This
was a radical message—and a dangerous
one—to publish in England at the time.*

SONNET XXXVI.

SHOULD the lone Wand'rer, fainting on his way,
　Rest for a moment of the sultry hours,
And tho' his path thro' thorns and roughnefs lay,
　Pluck the wild rose, or woodbine's gadding flow'rs;
Weaving gay wreaths, beneath some shelt'ring tree,
　The sense of sorrow, he awhile may lose;
So have I sought thy flow'rs, fair Poesy!
　So charm'd my way, with Friendship and the Muse.
But darker now grows Life's unhappy day,
　Dark, with new clouds of evil yet to come,
Her pencil sickening Fancy throws away,
　And weary Hope reclines upon the tomb;
And points my wishes to that tranquil shore,
Where the pale spectre Care, pursues no more.

Her pencil sickening fancy throws away
And weary hope reclines upon the tomb.

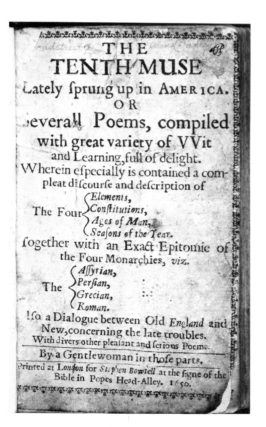

COLONIAL MUSIC

The earliest music in America was primarily religious. Every religious denomination (except the Quakers) called for some kind of music as a part of its religious services. In the early Puritan meetinghouses of New England, worshipers sang psalms to simple melodies, without any accompanying instrument. In the churches of the southern colonies, organs and organists occasionally appeared, imported from Europe. In the Moravian Church music was important and well performed. The Moravians were Protestant refugees from Europe who settled in Pennsylvania and North Carolina in the mid-1700s.

But church music did not remain America's only music for long. As early as 1729, European musicians began traveling to America and performing in public. The development of theater, particularly musicals, also contributed to the development of music in America. It was not until after the Revolution, however, that American music really began to thrive. By the turn of the century, the major American cities all had musical theaters, and concerts were given on a regular basis.

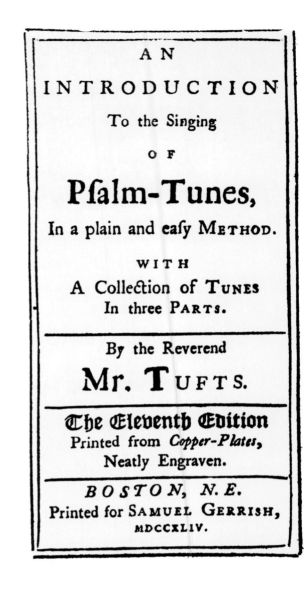

The Introduction to the Singing of Psalm-Tunes, *by the Reverend Mr. Tufts, was first published in Boston in 1721. It was one of the earliest American books of musical instruction, and the title page of the eleventh edition is proof of its popularity. Tufts's book was one of several that were written to teach Puritan worshipers the "regular" method of singing, so that the words of the psalms they sang could be better understood.*

"The Anacreontic Song" was a popular British drinking song. It was named for the ancient Greek poet Anacreon, who was known for his love of wine. Francis Scott Key used its melody for the verses he wrote during the British attack on Fort McHenry in 1814. The song, describing the sight of the "star-spangled banner" still flying over the fort after a night of heavy bombardment, became the official American national anthem in 1931. However, its bloodthirsty second and third verses, which celebrate Britain's defeat, are rarely sung, out of courtesy to a nation that is now one of America's closest allies.

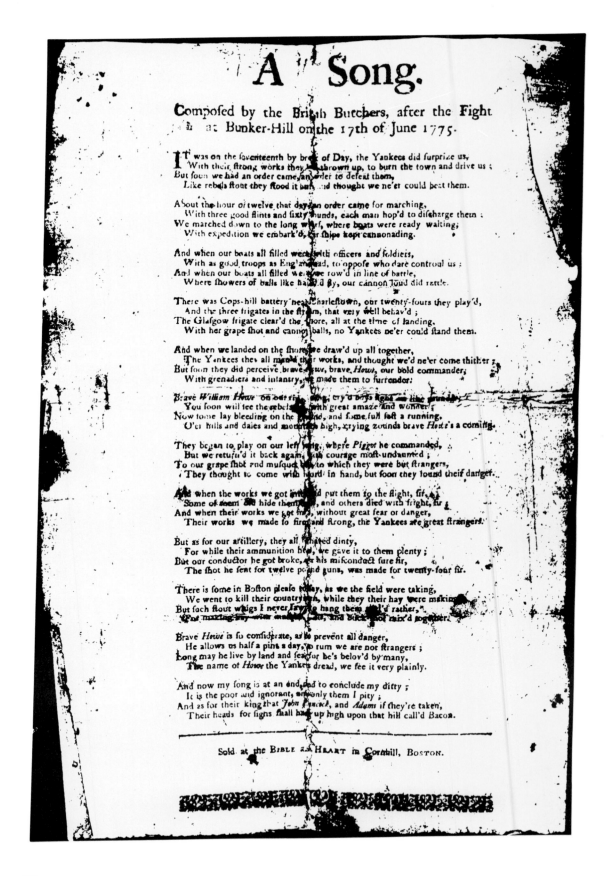

A Song.

Composed by the British Butchers, after the Fight at Bunker-Hill on the 17th of June 1775.

IT was on the seventeenth by break of Day, the Yankees did surprize us,
  With their strong works they had thrown up, to burn the town and drive us ;
But soon we had an order came, an order to defeat them,
  Like rebels stout they stood it out, and thought we ne'er could beat them.

About the hour of twelve that day an order came for marching,
  With three good flints and sixty rounds, each man hop'd to discharge them :
We marched down to the long wharf, where boats were ready waiting,
  With expedition we embark'd, our ships kept cannonading.

And when our boats all filled were, with officers and soldiers,
  With as good troops as England had, to oppose who dare controul us :
And when our boats all filled were, we row'd in line of battle,
  Where showers of balls like hail did fly, our cannon loud did rattle.

There was Cops-hill battery near Charlestown, our twenty-fours they play'd,
  And the three frigates in the stream, that very well behav'd ;
The Glasgow frigate clear'd the shore, all at the time of landing,
  With her grape shot and cannon balls, no Yankees ne'er could stand them.

And when we landed on the shore, we draw'd up all together,
  The Yankees they all mann'd their works, and thought we'd ne'er come thither ;
But soon they did perceive brave Howe, brave Howe, our bold commander,
  With grenadiers and infantry, we made them to surrender.

Brave William Howe on our right wing, cry'd boys fight on like thunder,
  You soon will see the rebels fly, with great amaze and wonder ;
Now some lay bleeding on the ground, and some full fast a running,
  O'er hills and dales and mountains high, crying zounds brave Howe's a coming.

They began to play on our left wing, where Pigot he commanded,
  But we return'd it back again, with courage most undaunted ;
To our grape shot and musquet balls, to which they were but strangers,
  They thought to come with sword in hand, but soon they found their danger.

And when the works we got into, and put them to the flight, sir,
  Some of them did hide themselves, and others died with fright, sir,
And when their works we got into, without great fear or danger,
  Their works we made so firm and strong, the Yankees are great strangers.

But as for our artillery, they all behaved dirty,
  For while their ammunition held, we gave it to them plenty ;
But our conductor he got broke, for his misconduct sure sir,
  The shot he sent for twelve pound guns, was made for twenty-four sir.

There is some in Boston please to say, as we the field were taking,
  We went to kill their countrymen, while they their hay were making,
But such stout whigs I never saw, to hang them all I'd rather,
  For making hay with musket balls, and buck shot mix'd together.

Brave Howe is so considerate, as to prevent all danger,
  He allows us half a pint a day, to rum we are not strangers ;
Long may he live by land and sea, for he's belov'd by many,
  The name of Howe the Yankees dread, we see it very plainly.

And now my song is at an end, and to conclude my ditty ;
  It is the poor and ignorant, and only them I pity ;
And as for their king that John Hancock, and Adams if they're taken,
  Their heads for signs shall hang up high upon that hill call'd Beacon.

Sold at the BIBLE and HEART in Cornhill, BOSTON.

Like every war, the Revolutionary War spawned many popular songs. "A Song, Composed by the British Butchers, after the Fight at Bunker-Hill on the 17th of June 1775" (opposite page), though strangely titled, celebrated a British victory, while "Yankee Doodle" (left) rallied the Patriots.

This illustration (below), from Denis Diderot's Encyclopédie, published in France between 1751 and 1772, shows craftsmen making brass instruments. This famous French encyclopedia's aim was to show the principle behind every art and science. The illustrations were of exceptional quality, and helped spread technical knowledge, such as how musical instruments were made. By the late eighteenth century, musical instruments—both imported or American-made—were widely available in America.

THE THEATER IN COLONIAL AMERICA

The first theatrical performances in the American colonies were given in the early eighteenth century, but it took most of that century to establish theater firmly as a part of American culture. European influence was strong in America, and most of the plays that were performed—and many of the actors who performed in them— were not Americans but Englishmen. Like many other arts, the first American drama developed only after the Revolutionary War, when Americans found a cause—liberty—worthy of enthusiastic celebration on the stage.

Drama prospered first in the southern colonies. In Charleston, South Carolina, the Dock Street Theater was established in the 1730s and featured the popular English tragedies and comedies of the day. Several theaters were established in New York in the mid-1700s. Even in Philadelphia—where a large Quaker population frowned on theatrical frivolities—a stage was built around the same time. Because the Puritans generally considered plays frivolous, theater came late to New England: Boston's first theater was built in the 1790s.

A

VAUDEVIL,

Sung by the Characters at the Conclusion of a new Farce, called the

BOSTON BLOCKADE.

TRUMORE.

YE Critics, who wait for an End of the Scene,
T' accept it with Praise or difmifs it with Spleen ;
Your Candour we afk and demand your Applaufe,
If not for our Action, at leaft for our Caufe.
'Tis our Aim by Amufement thus chearful and gay,
To wile a few Hours of Winter away :
While we reft on our Arms, call the Arts to our Aid,
And be merry in Spite of the BOSTON BLOCKADE.
CHORUS. 'Tis our Aim by &c. &c. &c.

MARIA.

YE Ladies, who find the Time hang on your Hands
While thus kept in a Cage by the Enemy's Bands :
Like me chufe a Mate from your numerous Crew,
Be he brave as my Soldier, as tender and true
With fuch a Kompanion Confinement has Charms ;
Each Place is a Paradife clafp'd in his Arms .
And only of Abfence and Difiance afraid,
You'll blefs the fmall Circle of BOSTON BLOCKADE.
CHO. With fuch a &c. &c. &c.

FANFAN.

YOUR Pardon my Maffa s one Word to intrude,
I'm fure in my Heart you won't all tink me rude :
Tho' in Public you fcoff, I fee many a Spark,
Woud tink me a fweet pretty Girl in the Dark.
Thus merily runs the World on with *Fanfan,*
I eat good falt Pork and get kifs'd by white Man :
I do Miffes Bufinefs, fhe pleas'd and I paid,
Egad I no tir'd of BOSTON BLOCKADE.
CHO. Thus merily runs &c. &c. &c.

DOODLE.

YE tarbarrell'd Lawgivers, yankified Prigs,
Who are Tyrants in Cuftom, yet call yourfelves Whigs :
In return for the Favours you've lavifh'd on me,
May I fee you all hang'd upon *Liberty Tree.*
Mean Time take Example, deceafe from Attack,
You're as week under Arms as I'm weak in my Back.
In War and in Love we alike are betray d,
And alike are the Laughter of BOSTON BLOCKADE.
CHO. Mean Time take &. &c. &c.

HEARTWRIGHT

COME round then ye Comrades of Honour and Truth,
Experienc'd Age and high-fpirited Youth ;
With Drum and with Fife make the Chorus more fhrill,
And Echo fhall waft it to WASHINGTON's Hill.
All brave BRITISH Hearts fhall beat Time while we fing,
Due Force to our Arms, and Long Life to the KING.
To the Honour of both be our Banners difplay'd,
And a glorious End to the BOSTON BLOCKADE.

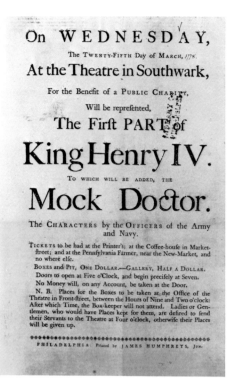

On WEDNESDAY,
The TWENTY-FIFTH Day of MARCH, 1778.
At the Theatre in Southwark,
For the Benefit of a PUBLIC CHARITY,
Will be reprefented,
The Firft PART of
King Henry IV.
To WHICH WILL BE ADDED, THE
Mock Doctor.
The CHARACTERS by the OFFICERS of the Army
and Navy.

TICKETS to be had at the Printer's; at the Coffee-houfe in Market-
ftreet; and at the Pennfylvania Farmer, near the New-Market, and
no where elfe.

BOXES and PIT, ONE DOLLAR.—GALLERY, HALF A DOLLAR.

Doors to open at Five o'Clock, and begin precifely at Seven.

No Money will, on any Account, be taken at the Door.

N. B. Places for the Boxes to be taken at the Office of the
Theatre in Front-ftreet, between the Hours of Nine and Two o'clock:
After which Time, the Box-keeper will not attend. Ladies or Gentlemen, who would have Places kept for them, are defired to fend
their Servants to the Theatre at Four o'clock, otherwife their Places
will be given up.

PHILADELPHIA: Printed by JAMES HUMPHREYS, Jun.

PONTEACH:
OR THE
Savages of America.
A
TRAGEDY.

Rogers, Robert

LONDON:
Printed for the Author; and Sold by J. MILLAN,
oppofite the Admiralty, Whiteball.
M.DCC.LXVI.
[Price 2 s. 6 d.]

This announcement (above, left) describes a performance of Shakespeare's Henry IV. Shakespearian drama was popular in the American colonies.

This tragedy, Ponteach: or the Savages of America *(above, right), was written by Major Robert Rogers in 1766. "Ponteach," better known as Pontiac, was a chief of the Ottawa Indians. He helped lead a rebellion against the British from 1763 to 1766, at the end of the French and Indian War.* Ponteach *was the first American play to be written about Indians.*

This theater, labeled "The John Street Theater" (below), is actually a London stage, but American stages were closely copied from English theaters.

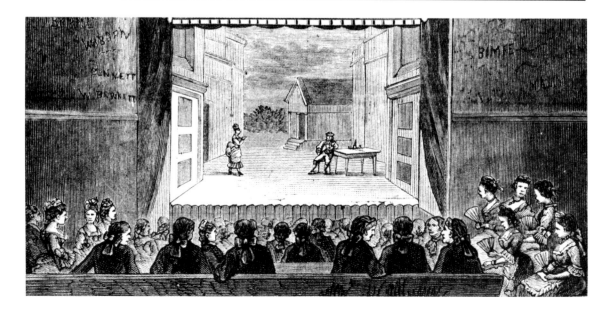

On Monday,

The SIXTEENTH Inſtant, *February 1778.*

At the Theatre in Southwark,

For the Benefit of a PUBLIC CHARITY,

Will be repreſented a Comedy

CALLED THE

Conſtant Couple.

TO WHICH WILL BE ADDED,

DUKE AND NO DUKE.

The CHARACTERS by the OFFICERS of the ARMY and NAVY.

TICKETS to be had at the Printer's: at the Coffee-houſe in Market-ſtreet: and at the Pennſilvania Farmer, near the New-Market, and no where elſe.

BOXES and PIT, ONE DOLLAR.—GALLERY, HALF A DOLLAR.

Doors to open at Five o'Clock, and begin preciſely at Seven.

No Money will, on any Account, be taken at the Door.

Gentlemen are earneſtly requeſted not to attempt to bribe the Door-keepers.

. N. B. Places for the Boxes to be taken at the Office of the Theatre in Front-ſtreet, between the Hours of Nine and Two o'clock: After which Time, the Box-keeper will not attend. Ladies or Gentlemen, who would have Places kept for them, are deſired to ſend their Servants to the Theatre at Four o'clock, otherwiſe their Places will be given up.

PHILADELPHIA. PRINTED BY JAMES HUMPHREYS, JUNR.

Philadelphia's Chestnut Street Theatre (above) opened in 1794. It was modeled after the Theatre Royal in Bath, England, and its superior design made it a landmark in the development of theater in America. This engraving was made by William Birch, who emigrated from England to America in 1794 and settled in Philadelphia. In 1800, he published a set of "Views" of his adopted city.

This announcement (left) describes the performance of two comedies, The Constant Couple and Duke and No Duke. The plays were staged in Philadelphia in February 1778 for the benefit of an unidentified charity. The players were local army and navy officers. A line near the bottom of the notice, "Gentlemen are earnestly requested not to attempt to bribe the Door-keepers," gives some flavor of the theater of the time.

This etching shows one view of a design for a new theater to be built in Richmond, Virginia. The designs were made from 1797 to 1798 by Benjamin Henry Latrobe, one of the finest architects of the early American period. In this design, he was greatly influenced by his broad knowledge of European theaters. Although Richmond's existing theater burned down a few weeks after these drawings were completed, money to build the new theater was never raised.

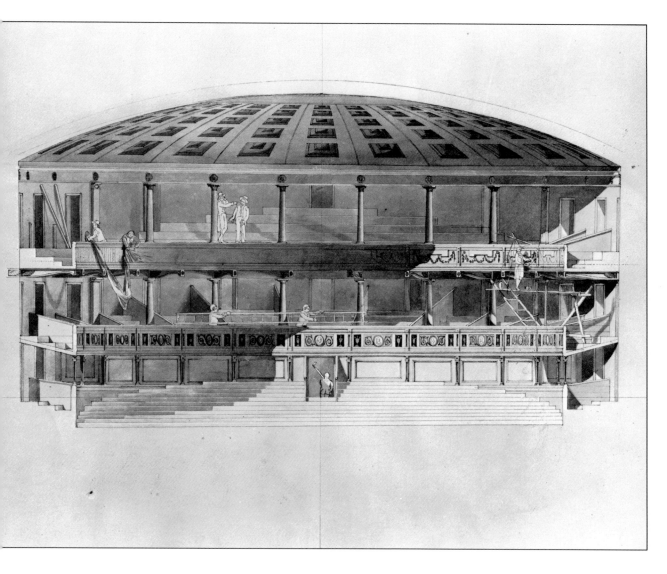

AMERICAN HOMES BY COLONIAL ARCHITECTS

The first settlers in America struggled to provide adequate shelter against the harsh climate of their new land. They lived in dugouts, cabins, and in wigwams adopted from the Indians.

As the colonies prospered, however, people began to build more graceful houses. Most were designed by amateur architects and were built of wood because it was a cheap, plentiful material. After about 1750, new architectural ideas began to spread, and the Georgian style, already popular in England, was soon introduced. In America, Georgian buildings—formal, symmetrical and usually built of brick—were strongly influenced by the work of Sir Christopher Wren, one of England's foremost architects. Wren, in turn, had been heavily influenced by the work of the Italian Renaissance architect Andrea Palladio (1508–80).

In the late 1700s, the first professional architects from Europe arrived in America. From this period on, American architecture no longer lagged behind European styles but quickly adapted them into a distinctive American style.

This engraving (above) shows the "Slate Roof House," an important example of early Philadelphia architecture. The house was built for Samuel Carpenter, a successful merchant, probably in 1687. It was designed by a British architect—unusual for the time. Its slate roof and formal, H-shaped design is one of the marks of the Renaissance architectural style that was becoming popular in America. Unfortunately, the house was destroyed in 1867.

This drawing (below) shows the house of Paul Revere, the famous silversmith whose midnight ride warned the American rebels of British troop movements on April 18, 1775. The house, in Boston's North Square, was near the Old North Church, where the lanterns ("one if by land, two if by sea") that would signal British troop movements were hung. The original structure of the Revere house was probably built by John Jeffs in the late seventeenth century. By the time Revere occupied it in 1770, the original two-story house had grown into a building of three stories. Although it later deteriorated badly, it was restored to its late-seventeenth-century state in 1908.

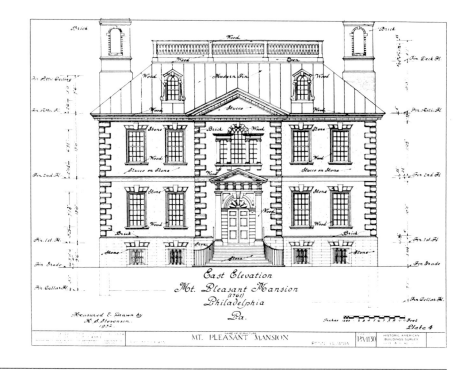

Mount Pleasant, a mansion built by John Macpherson in Philadelphia in 1761-62, is shown here in this elevation or architectural drawing (above). Macpherson was a wealthy Scottish sea captain, and his house is one of the most elaborate of those in the late Georgian style. The tall, arched window above the door, with a flat-topped window at either side, is a typical Palladian element, and the triangular pediments over the door and at the roofline are characteristic Georgian touches. The house was sold to Benedict Arnold in 1779, but he occupied it for only a short time before he betrayed his country and escaped to England.

This engraving (below) shows Mount Airy, a formal mansion built for Colonel John Taylor in Richmond County, Virginia, between 1758 and 1762. Mount Airy is another outstanding house in the late Georgian style. It was designed by John Ariss, one of the few professional architects of the time, and is built of stone—unusual in Virginia at the time. It seems to have been copied from The Book of Architecture, by the Englishman James Gibbs, one of Ariss's primary sources throughout his career.

T H E

BRITISH ARCHITECT:

OR, THE

BUILDERS TREASURY

O F

STAIR-CASES.

CONTAINING.

I. An Easier, more intelligible, and expeditious METHOD of drawing the FIVE ORDERS, than has hitherto been publish'd, by a SCALE of Twelve equal Parts, free from those troublesome Divisions, call'd *Aliquot Parts*. Shewing also how to glue up their COLUMNS and CAPITALS.

II. Likewise STAIR CASES, (those most useful, ornamental, and necessary Parts of a BUILDING, though never before sufficiently described in any Book, Ancient or Modern;) shewing their most convenient Situation, and the Form of their Ascending in the most grand Manner: With a great Variety of curious ORNAMENTS, whereby any Gentleman may fix on what will suit him best, there being EXAMPLES of all Kinds; and necessary DIRECTIONS for such Persons as are unacquainted with that BRANCH.

III. DESIGNS of ARCHES, DOORS, and WINDOWS.

IV. A great Variety of New and Curious CHIMNEY-PIECES, in the most elegant and modern TASTE.

V. CORBELS, SHIELDS, and other beautiful DECORATIONS.

VI. Several useful and necessary RULES of CARPENTRY, with the Manner of TRUSS'D ROOFS, and the Nature of a splay'd circular SOFFIT, both in a straight and Circular Wall, never published before. Together with Raking CORNICES, GROINS, and ANGLE BRACKETS described.

The Whole being illustrated with upwards of One Hundred Designs and Examples, curiously engraved on Sixty Folio Copper-Plates.

By ABRAHAM SWAN, ARCHITECT.

PHILADELPHIA.

Printed by R. BELL, Bookseller, *Third-Street*, next Door to *St. Paul's* Church, For JOHN NORMAN ARCHITECT ENGRAVER, in *Second-Street*.

M, DCC, LXXV.

The British Architect *(above)*, *published in Philadelphia in 1775, promised American architects "upwards of One Hundred Designs and Examples" of various architectural features, including "Stair Cases (those most useful, ornamental, and necessary Parts of a Building, though never before sufficiently described in any Book, Ancient or Modern)." Books like this played an important part in publicizing new architectural styles throughout the colonies.*

John Carlyle was a Scottish merchant who emigrated to America in 1740. He became a prominent citizen of Alexandria, Virginia. In 1755, General Edward Braddock and five colonial governors met at his house, shown in this architectural drawing (left), to plan a campaign against the French and Indians. George Washington, a colonel at the time, was also present.

WEST ELEVATION
(CONJECTURAL RESTORATION)

Mount Vernon (top), the home of George Washington, began as a small farmhouse built in the mid-1730s. It came into George Washington's possession in 1754, and three years later he began extensive renovations. The renovations continued, in three main spurts, over the next thirty years, until Washington finally considered the house finished in 1787. John Ariss may have been the architect of the first two sets of renovations, in 1757–58 and 1773–79.

This design (bottom) for a group of Boston town houses, called the Tontine Crescent, was published in Massachusetts Magazine in February 1794. These town houses were very different from formal mansions like Mount Airy and Mount Pleasant. The architect, Charles Bulfinch (1763–1844), began the project in 1793, but only the southern crescent was completed before funding ran out. Bulfinch also designed the Massachusetts State House on Boston's Beacon Hill.

PLACES OF WORSHIP

Many settlers came to America for religious reasons, and churches were architecturally important from the earliest colonial days. One of the buildings the *Mayflower* Pilgrims built during their first winter was a meetinghouse, and thereafter the simple, undecorated style of the Puritan meetinghouse dominated early New England church architecture.

In the Southern colonies, most settlers belonged to the Church of England. Sometimes they sought to reproduce the Gothic style of the churches that they had known in England, but often their early churches were also plain. Unlike the square meetinghouses, they were usually the traditional rectangular shape with an altar at one end.

More elaborate American churches began to appear in the early 1700s. Brick, and occasionally stone, was used more often in place of wood. Churches formed in the shape of a cross began to replace plain rectangular churches and square meetinghouses. Steeples, spires, and towers appeared, as did larger, more ornamental windows.

King's Chapel (above) was built in Boston by architect Peter Harrison between 1749 and 1754. Harrison was one of the finest architects in the colonies, and King's Chapel is an impressive example of his work. The large blocklike tower that dominates the church was meant to support an elaborate spire, but that was never built. The exterior of the church is therefore less impressive than the interior, where Corinthian columns stand in stately pairs down the nave to an altar lit by a graceful Palladian window.

St. Paul's Chapel (below), built in New York City from 1764 to 1766, was designed by Thomas McBean, a Scottish architect. The spire of the chapel was the tallest in the colonies when it was built. Working from James Gibbs's Book of Architecture, McBean modeled St. Paul's after a design for a church in London. Today St. Paul's is the only surviving church in New York that was built before the Revolution.

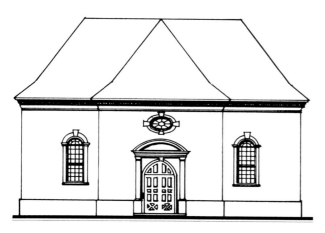

This drawing (left) shows the western elevation of Christ Church, built in Lancaster County, Virginia, in 1732. The architect is unknown, but may have been named John Prince. At any rate, the design seems to come from a British book of architectural plans patterned after those of Renaissance architect Andrea Palladio. The church's many fine details, such as the tall, narrow windows topped by rounded arches, and its pleasing proportions make it a fine example of a Georgian church.

This engraving of the interior of Christ Church (below) shows its fine walnut woodwork and beautiful interior design. The pine pews have high backs to keep off drafts, and above the altar the Ten Commandments are written. Some consider the church the finest example of eighteenth-century classical architecture in the United States.

PUBLIC BUILDINGS

Like churches, the first public and commercial buildings in the colonies were simple, functional structures built of wood. But as towns and cities prospered, citizens usually replaced their first civic buildings with sturdier and more substantial brick or stone buildings of increasingly elaborate design. Government and other public buildings reflected the wealth and taste of a particular city, and the greatest care was taken in designing and building them.

This engraving shows several views of Virginia's Capitol, in Williamsburg. Williamsburg was the capital of Virginia from 1699 to 1779 and boasts some of the finest architecture in all of the colonies. The Capitol was built from 1701 to 1705 according to a simple, functional plan. It contained a large hall and several smaller meeting rooms for Virginia's ruling body, the House of Burgesses, as well as the general court and an office for the governor. The building was destroyed by fire twice, and only its foundations were left when the restoration of colonial Williamsburg began in 1928. The nature illustrations at the bottom of this engraving indicate that this may have been the work of American naturalist John Bartram.

This engraving (below) shows Independence Hall, built in Philadelphia from 1732 to 1755. The building was originally called the State House, but it was renamed after the Declaration of Independence was signed there in 1776. Independence Hall was designed by Andrew Hamilton, Pennsylvania's Speaker of the Assembly, who had an amateur interest in architecture.

This Maryland state house (above) is actually the third state house built in Maryland. The first was built in 1676 in the settlement called Mary's City. After Annapolis was established as the new capital of the Maryland colony in 1694, St. Mary's was abandoned. Another state house was built in Annapolis in 1697 and was rebuilt after a fire in 1706. By the 1770s, however, it was in great disrepair, and the new state house pictured here replaced it in 1772.

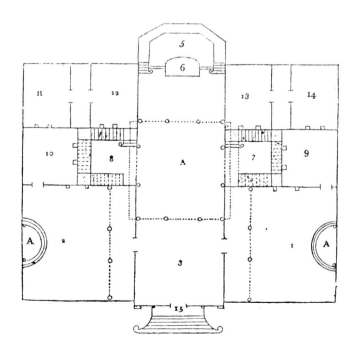

Maryland's new state house (left) was built under the direction of Joseph Clarke. The two-story building is designed around a central open area, and it is topped by a large dome with a spire on top. The dome was not part of the original design but was built in 1784.

Charleston's Exchange and Customs Building (above) was built from 1767 to 1771 according to the design of architect William Rigby Nagler. It was one of the most elaborate public buildings of the colonial era and marked the great prosperity of the growing city of Charleston. The Exchange originally had an open arcade all around it, but this was later closed in. Much of the building's original decoration was also removed at a later date.

New York's Old City Hall (left) was built in 1699–1700. The building was renovated extensively after the Revolutionary War and became known as Federal Hall. The original building was a mix of colonial and Georgian styles. It was on the steps of this building that George Washington was inaugurated as the first president of the United States, in 1789.

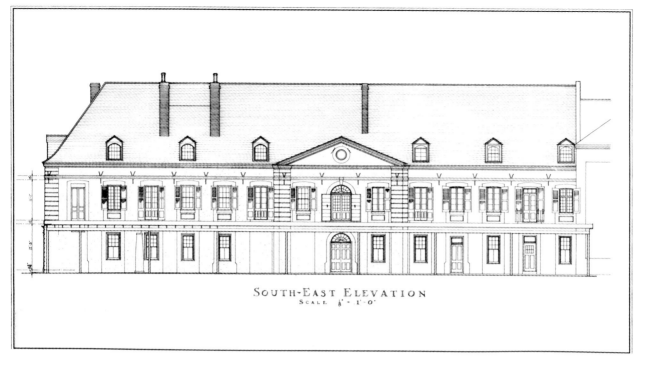

SOUTH-EAST ELEVATION
SCALE ⅛" = 1'-0"

The city of New Orleans had been ruled by two nations (Spain and France) before finally becoming part of the United States after the Louisiana Purchase, in 1803. Because of its international heritage, New Orleans was home to buildings of varied architectural styles. Major fires in 1788 and 1794, however, destroyed many of these buildings. One that survives is the Ursuline Convent (above), completed in 1750, which served as a residence for members of a Roman Catholic religious order and later as an orphanage.

The San José mission (left), founded in San Antonio, Texas, in the 1740s, is one of the best examples of Spanish colonial architecture. It was fortified against attacks, with very few windows facing the exterior plaza. Instead, the eighty-four apartments built for Christianized Indians, a few soldiers' quarters, and the church overlook an interior courtyard. The geometric patterns in the stucco exterior, as well as the beautifully carved designs bordering the main front window, are in the Spanish Baroque style.

Part II
The Sciences

This illustration from the Universal Magazine *(published in London but popular in America) shows an experiment to discover the effects of electricity on a cat, a bird, a plant, and several inanimate objects.*

Early Americans were very interested in the sciences. This was a natural result of the challenges of settling a new land, which Americans tackled with energy and enthusiasm. While ordinary citizens carved farms and cities out of the wilderness, explorers traveled through vast expanses of uncharted territory. They brought back descriptions and sketches of new and different plants and animals, as well as of the American Indians and their ways of life.

Americans were interested most of all in the practical sciences. The discovery of new kinds of plants meant an opportunity to open new markets—tobacco and cotton, for instance. New plants also offered an opportunity to cross seeds from Europe with those of America to produce healthier or more productive varieties. While European scientists had been experimenting with electricity for years, it was Benjamin Franklin who found the first practical application for this new knowledge: the lightning rod.

Many early American scientists, particularly physicians, were trained in Europe. But many others taught themselves, studying whatever books they could find—usually imported from England and Europe. These self-taught scientists were part of a proud tradition of self-sufficiency. With the growth of cities and towns, however, Americans began to build universities, and also hospitals. By the mid-eighteenth century, America was training its own scientists and doctors and had started on the road to scientific excellence.

MARK CATESBY

The earliest book on the natural history of America was *Joyfull Newes out of the New Founde World*, published in London in 1577. This book was about the plants of the Carolinas, and it aroused an early interest in New World plants among the English. Mark Catesby (born in England about 1679) first traveled to America in 1712. He returned to England in 1719 but traveled back to America in 1722 to make a formal study of the natural history of the southern colonial territories. Catesby did not have much formal training, but his 220 etchings—nearly half of them of birds, and all of them colored by hand—were accurate and significantly increased the knowledge of America's natural history.

Catesby's Natural History of Carolina, Florida and the Bahama Islands *(above) was published in London in 1731. It was the result of his three-year study of those regions and introduced their "Birds, Beasts, Fishes, Serpents, Insects, and Plants" to an enthusiastic European audience.*

This Catesby etching (left) shows a bird called the tufted titmouse, standing on a branch of a water tupelo tree. Titmice are small birds related to chickadees. The tupelo tree, or black gum, is native to eastern North America.

Shown here is Cateby's illustration of the powerful and stately bald eagle, which was adopted by the founders of our nation as the national emblem in 1782. Since that time, it has appeared on virtually every official seal and document of the United States.

Catesby shows the anemia snake curled elaborately upon itself next to a lillium plant. The plant belongs to the lily family, which also includes irises and amaryllises.

THE TRAVELS OF PETER KALM

The Swedish naturalist Peter Kalm (1715–79) traveled through North America from 1748 to 1751, making a survey of the natural history of the territory. A three-volume account of his travels was published from 1753 to 1761. Kalm was a friend of another famous Swedish botanist, Carolus Linnaeus. It was Linnaeus who invented the modern system of classifying plants and animals in groups according to their characteristics. This science is known as taxonomy. In the Linnaean system, every living thing is given a unique name consisting of two, or sometimes three, Latin words. The first word identifies the genus, or general group, to which a plant or animal belongs, and the second identifies it as a particular species within that group. If a third name is used, it identifies a variety or race of the species. This system of classification was the one used to identify all the new kinds of plants and animals discovered in America.

TRAVELS

INTO

NORTH AMERICA;

CONTAINING

Its NATURAL HISTORY, AND

A circumſtantial Account of its Plantations and Agriculture in general,

WITH THE

CIVIL, ECCLESIASTICAL AND COMMERCIAL STATE OF THE COUNTRY,

The MANNERS of the INHABITANTS; and ſeveral curious and IMPORTANT REMARKS on various ſubjeƈts.

BY PETER KALM,

Profeſſor of Oeconomy in the Univerſity of *Aobo* in Swediſh *Finland,* and Member of the *Swediſh* Royal Academy of Sciences.

TRANSLATED INTO ENGLISH

BY JOHN REINHOLD FORSTER, F. A. S.

Enriched with a Map, ſeveral Cuts for the Illuſtration of Natural Hiſtory, and ſome additional Notes.

THE SECOND EDITION.

IN TWO VOLUMES,

VOL. I.

LONDON,

Printed for T. LOWNDES, Nᵒ 77, in Fleet-ſtreet. 1772.

This English translation of Peter Kalm's Travels into North America (above) was published in London in 1772. As the title explains, Kalm's book discussed not just the native plants and animals of the New World, but also its agriculture, its political and religious organization, and "the manners of the inhabitants."

Though the arrival of settlers in North America threatened the survival of many plant and animal inhabitants, the raccoon managed to adapt and flourish in the new man-made environment. A nocturnal, solitary animal, the raccoon was able to avoid colonial hunters, and its long, coarse fur protected it from the bitter cold winters of the colonies.

This map (above) shows part of the Gulf Stream, the strong current of warm water that runs from the Gulf of Mexico, past Florida, up the eastern coast of America to Newfoundland, and across the northern Atlantic Ocean. Benjamin Franklin commissioned the map in 1786 to help sailors shorten their journeys. Since the Gulf Stream moves at an average of four miles an hour, a slow-moving sailing vessel could gain a lot of speed by sailing with the current—and needlessly slow her voyage by sailing against it. This map was the first to show the Gulf Stream as one continuous current and the first to be widely distributed.

This map from Massachusetts Magazine shows the path that herring swim in the course of the year. These small fish were—and still are—an important food source. The map of their annual migration gave fishermen a useful tool in predicting the best place to fish at different times of the year.

PIONEERING AMERICAN BOTANISTS

John Bartram (1699–1777) is often called the father of American botany. He was the first native-born botanist and served England's King George III as the official botanist of the American colonies from 1765 on. Bartram's greatest contribution to the science of plants was his experimentation in hybridization—the crossing of plants to create seedlings that combine the characteristics of their parents. Bartram exported many seeds and plants from America to Europe, and he established a famous botanical garden in Philadelphia.

John Bartram's son William also became a botanist. Unlike his father, William was a gifted artist and captured the plants and creatures of the New World on paper with great skill. Both father and son were keen observers of their surroundings, and their descriptions of the various Indians they met in their travels are an important part of their legacy.

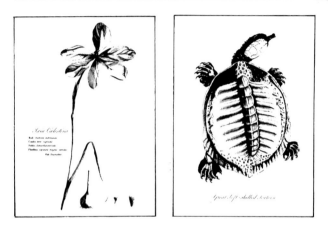

William Bartram published his Travels *(top) in 1791. His engaging literary style, keen observations, and numerous discoveries made the book a tremendous success. By 1799, it had been published in Britain, Ireland, the Netherlands, France, and Germany.*

William Bartram's engraving of the Ixia Coelestina *(above, left) shows an example of this large-blossomed plant, and by its side, an example of the bulb the flower grew from.*

Bartram described the great soft-shelled tortoise (above, right) as "very large when full grown, from twenty to thirty and forty pounds weight, [and] extremely delicious.... They are very flat and thin...in form, appearance, and texture, very much resembling the sea turtle."

This engraving by Antoine Dupratz (1689?–1775?; right) shows a Natchez Indian dressed in his winter clothing. Dupratz lived among the Natchez in Louisiana for eight years. His History of Louisiana, published in 1758, offered an account of the relationship between the French and the Indians in the area, as well as much other valuable information about the region.

This catalogue of the fruitful "Trees, Shrubs, and Herbacious Plants" (below) growing in John Bartram's famous botanical garden in Philadelphia gives a good indication of his energetic trade in American plants.

MEDICAL PRACTICE IN EARLY AMERICA

Before the 1600s, doctors were completely unable to prevent diseases. They could only attempt to cure them—sometimes with preposterous sounding mixtures or techniques. But the 1600s was a time of great progress in medicine. William Harvey discovered that the blood is circulated by the heart. And with the invention of the compound microscope—which combined two lenses for higher magnification—scientists were able to study details of the body's structure that had previously been invisible.

Medical knowledge, like any other knowledge that required extensive learning and training, had to be imported in early America. Most early physicians were either European-trained immigrants or Americans who traveled abroad for training. Few books, much less fancy instruments like microscopes, were available, and the first American doctors had to rely on books printed and published abroad. The first American medical schools were established in the mid-1700s, however, and after this, Americans began to make their own contributions to the store of medical knowledge.

This portrait of Cotton Mather (1663–1728) was made in 1727, the year before he died. Mather, a prominent Puritan minister, is often remembered for his role in the witchcraft trials in Salem. But Mather had a wide range of interests, including medicine. His support for the use of a vaccine against smallpox—a highly contagious and often fatal disease—helped gain acceptance for the use of vaccines.

The truly Learned and Honoᵇˡᵉ Sʳ Kenelme Digby Kᵗ Chancellor to the Q: Mother Aged 62.

Groffe fculpfit

Choice and Experimented

RECEIPTS

IN

Phyfick and Chirurgery,

AS ALSO

Cordial and Diftilled

Waters and Spirits, Perfumes,
and other Curiofities.

Collected by the Honourable
and truly Learned

Sir *KENELM DIGBY* Kt.

Chancellour to her Majefty the
QUEEN MOTHER.

Tranflated out of feveral Languages
by *G. H.*

London, Printed for the Author, and are to
be fold by *H. Brome* at the Star in
Litte-Britain, 1668.

This medical guide (above), by the "truly learned" Sir Kenelm Digby, was published in London in 1668. It contains "Receipts," or recipes, for the various medicines of the day. Such books were important in spreading medical knowledge throughout the colonies.

As the title page of Zabdiel Boylston's book about the smallpox vaccine explains, the book contains "some short directions to the unexperienced." Boylston began using the smallpox vaccine at the advice and with the encouragement of Cotton Mather. Together, Boylston and Mather persevered, although the vaccine was extremely unpopular: people feared it would give them the disease, not prevent it. This History is the last of several books written by Mather and Boylston on the subject and is the first presentation of a clinical experiment by an American physician. Boylston's careful records showed that the smallpox vaccine was indeed highly effective.

AN

Hiftorical ACCOUNT

OF THE

SMALL-POX

INOCULATED

IN

NEW ENGLAND,

Upon all Sorts of Perfons, *Whites, Blacks,*
and of all Ages and Conftitutions.

With fome Account of the Nature of the
Infection in the NATURAL and INOCULATED
Way, and their different Effects on HUMAN
BODIES.

With fome fhort DIRECTIONS to the UN-
EXPERIENCED in this Method of Practice.

Humbly dedicated to her Royal Highnefs the Princefs of WALES,

By *Zabdiel Boylfton,* F. R. S.

The Second Edition, Corrected.

LONDON:

Printed for S. CHANDLER, at the Crofs-Keys in the *Pultry.*
M. DCC. XXVI.

Re-Printed at *BOSTON* in *N. E.* for S. GERRISH in
Cornbil, and T. HANCOCK at the *Bible* and *Three Crowns*
in *Amfreet.* M. DCC. XXX.

SURGERY AND DENTISTRY

Early surgery was usually practiced by barbers, whose qualifications were sometimes little more than the possession of sharp instruments. Although surgeons began to receive formal training during the sixteenth century, most still possessed limited skills and training. There were no anesthetics, and the high rate of fatal post-surgical infections limited the usefulness of surgery in early America, just as in Europe.

Medical training was slightly more formal during the seventeenth century. Doctors studied anatomy, chemistry, and even botany but generally learned most of their skills as apprentices to practicing doctors. Surgical training was separate from medical training, but surgeons also studied the general sciences—anatomy in particular—and trained as apprentices. It was not until the discovery of germs and of anesthesia, both in the mid-nineteenth century, that surgery became a truly effective medical technique.

The ANATOMY of Man's Body, as governed by the Twelve CONSTELLATIONS.

♈ The Head and Face.

♊ Arms · ♌ Heart · ♎ Reins · ♐ Thighs · ♒ Legs

♉ Neck · ♋ Breaſt · ♍ Bowels · ♏ Secrets · ♑ Knees

♓ The Feet.

To know where the Sign is

Firſt Find the Day of the Month, and againſt the Day you have the Sign or place of the Moon in the 6th Column. Then finding the Sign here, it ſhews the part of the Body it governs.

The Names and Characters of the Seven Planets

☉ Sol, ♄ Saturn, ♃ Jupiter, ♂ Mars, ♀ Venus, ☿ Mercury, ☽ Luna, ☊ Dragon's head, and ☋ tail.

The Five Aspects.

☌ Conjunction, ☍ Oppoſition, ✳ Sextile, △ Trine, □ Quartile.

This illustration from Benjamin Franklin's Poor Richard's Almanack (above) charts the influence that certain planets and stars were thought to have on different parts of the body. The medical knowledge of the day was one part science and another part unscientific guesswork, like this chart.

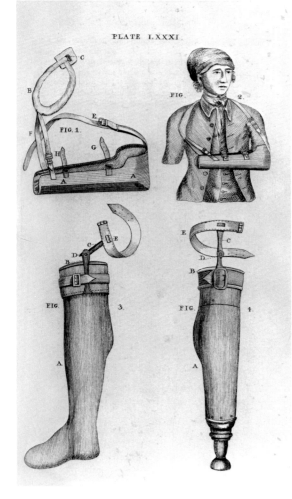

This Dutch woodcut (above), made during the eighteenth century, shows a street dentist at work on his patient. Although dentistry became a separate science in England in the seventeenth century, the earliest American dentists were barber-surgeons. Some early dentists were trained in the full medical and surgical learning of the day, but street dentists like this one rarely had much training. The first American dental textbooks appeared by the beginning of the eighteenth century, and the first American dental school opened in Baltimore in 1840.

This plate (right) is from Benjamin Bell's A System of Surgery, a British medical manual widely used in America. Much in American medicine was drawn from British and Scottish precepts and practices.

THE REVOLUTIONARY WAR AND MEDICINE

The Revolutionary War, like all wars, created a tremendous need for doctors. Since doctors were already in short supply in America, and since the nature of war was that wounded soldiers were often kept in unhygienic conditions, even a small battle wound could result in death.

At the request of George Washington, the Continental Congress organized the first military hospital in July 1775, after the siege of Boston. The first director general of military hospitals was Benjamin Church, but he was quickly dismissed when he was discovered to be a traitor to the American cause.

Church was succeeded by John Morgan and then by William Shippen. Both were distinguished American physicians and founders of the first American medical school, in Philadelphia in 1765. Neither man was able to bring much order to the practice of military medicine, however. Benjamin Rush, perhaps the most famous of all early American physicians, was made surgeon-general of the armies in April 1777. But he found conditions so terrible and resistance to improvements so strong that he soon resigned in protest, accusing Dr. Shippen of mismanagement.

Only with the appointment of John Cochrane as director general in 1781 did military hospitals begin to achieve any real degree of organization.

This engraving (above) shows John Cochrane, who volunteered his services to the American army in 1776. Dr. Cochrane had served as a surgeon's mate in the hospital department of the British army during the French and Indian War and had learned much about military hospitals. As a friend of George Washington's, he was appointed a physician and surgeon-general of the army in April 1777 and later became the chief physician and surgeon. Like Benjamin Rush, Cochrane was dismayed by medical conditions during the war. His promotion to director-general of American hospitals in 1781 put him in a good position to improve conditions.

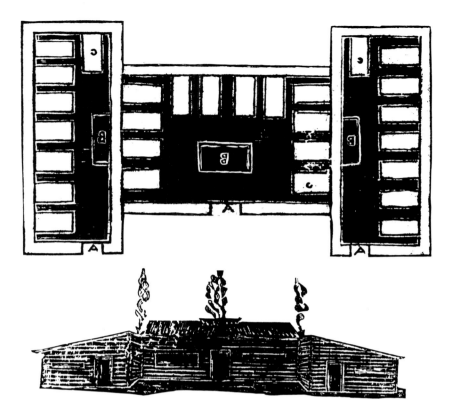

These drawings show the design for a log-hewn hospital hut used during the Revolutionary War. The design for the hospital was based on a traditional Indian building.

This engraving shows the instruments of a Revolutionary War surgeon. Unfortunately, surgeons of the day didn't know that germs caused infections, and the use of dirty instruments was a leading cause of surgical complications and even death.

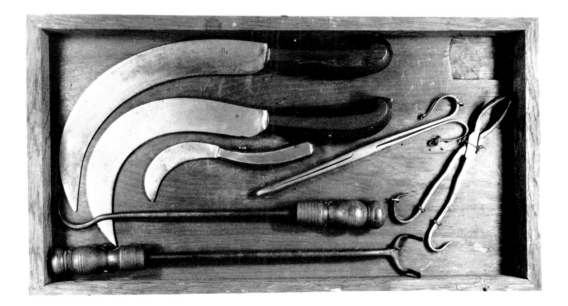

MEDICINE: PHILADELPHIA AND BOSTON

As cities and towns grew, hospitals were built. In Philadelphia, the Friends' Almshouse was built in 1732. New York built a public workhouse, whose infirmary developed into Bellevue Hospital, in 1734. In 1736, St. Philip's Hospital was founded in Charleston. All these early hospitals were primarily for the care of the poor, especially the mentally ill. The first general hospital, Pennsylvania Hospital in Philadelphia, was not established until 1751.

As in England, most early American hospitals were run privately, not by the government. They reflected a strong social purpose more than a formal scientific effort to improve medical practice in the country. But hospitals did offer improvements in patient care. Perhaps more importantly, they helped to improve medical education, training, and research by centralizing medical services. By the end of the eighteenth century hospitals had become a vital part of the practice of medicine in America.

Benjamin Rush was one of the most prominent eighteenth-century American physicians. After five years of apprenticeship under notable Philadelphia physicians, Rush earned a doctor's degree from the University of Edinburgh in 1768, and also trained in a London hospital. Rush's interests were broad. As a member of the Continental Congress, he signed the Declaration of Independence. He was an outspoken opponent of slavery. He was one of the earliest scientists to connect yellow fever with unsanitary conditions, and as a professor at the College of Philadelphia (later the University of Pennsylvania) he trained thousands of new American physicians.

The Massachusetts Medical Society (left) was one of the earliest medical societies in America. It was founded in 1781 and began publishing its proceedings in 1790. Once American doctors began to form their own organizations, they were better able to promote medical knowledge and technologies.

The Massachusetts General Hospital (below, center) was designed by Charles Bulfinch in the 1790s but was not actually built until 1820. The hospital today is one of the finest centers of medical training in the country.

This etching (bottom) shows Philadelphia's Pennsylvania Hospital. It was founded in 1751 and opened the next year. The first general hospital in America, Pennsylvania Hospital was organized by Benjamin Franklin and Benjamin Rush.

THE RISE OF SCIENTIFIC LEARNING

The work of the English scientists Isaac Newton (1642–1727) and Robert Boyle (1627–91) put scientific learning on a whole new footing in the seventeenth century. Newton's laws of gravity became a basis of modern physics. Robert Boyle's discoveries about chemical elements and chemical reactions, as well as his laws about the nature of gases, helped to establish the modern science of chemistry.

Experiments, not vague theories, were the currency of the scientists of the day, and Americans contributed their efforts with enthusiasm. Benjamin Franklin is one of the best-known early American scientists. But science was still a general field, and Americans at every level of education were interested in and able to contribute to scientific learning. The American Philosophical Society for Promoting Useful Knowledge was founded in 1769 in Philadelphia, with Benjamin Franklin as its first president. This society—the oldest scientific society in America—contributed greatly to the advancement of American science. The society's full name, with its emphasis on *useful* knowledge, is a good illustration of the attitude toward scientific study that prevailed at the time.

These engravings (above), from the French Encyclopédie *by Denis Diderot, show an eighteenth-century laboratory and a selection of containers for conducting chemical experiments. The study of chemistry made great advances in the eighteenth century, when grand theories of alchemy were abandoned in favor of proper chemical experiments.*

PREMIUMS.

THE AMERICAN PHILOSOPHICAL SOCIETY,

HELD AT PHILADELPHIA, FOR PROMOTING USEFUL KNOWLEDGE,

IN order the more effectually to answer the ends of their institution, have agreed to appropriate, annually, a part of their funds to be disposed of in Premiums to the Authors of the best performances, inventions, or improvements, relative to certain specific subjects of useful knowledge. The following premiums, therefore, are now proposed by the Society.

I.

For the best system of liberal education and literary instruction, adapted to the genius of the government, and best calculated to promote the general welfare, of the United States; comprehending also a plan for instituting and conducting public schools, in this country, on principles of the most extensive utility.——*A premium of one hundred dollars.*
Papers on this subject will be received, till the first day of January, 1797.

II.

For the most simple, easy and expeditious method of computing the longitude, from the common lunar observation,——*A premium of seventy dollars.*
The particular view of the society, in proposing this subject, is, that the solution of this most useful problem may, if possible, be rendered so plain and easy, as to be readily learned by every mariner, even of moderate capacity, who understands the common rules of arithmetic; and thus be introduced into general practice.
Papers on this subject will be received, till the first day of January, 1797.

III.

For the best construction or improvement of ship-pumps,——*A premium of seventy dollars.*
Improvements which may be readily applied to the ship-pumps in common use, will be most likely to be adopted by seamen, and introduced into general practice.
Papers on this subject will be received, till the first day of January, 1797.

IV.

For the best construction or improvement of stoves, or fire-places,——*A premium of sixty dollars.* The principal end which the society have in view, in proposing this subject, is the benefit of the poorer class of people, especially of such as live in towns, or other places where fuel is dear. To answer this end, the stove should be cheap, and of durable materials; should afford the necessary degree of a salubrious and durable heat, with the least expence of fuel possible; and should be capable of being employed both for the purpose of warming the room, and cooking provisions for the family.——The society have been informed, that stoves made of brick are, in many respects, superior to those made of metal; especially, in the saving of fuel, and preserving a more equable degree of heat.
Papers on this subject will be received, till the first day of January, 1797.

V.

For the best method, verified by experiment, of preventing the premature decay of Peach-trees,——*A premium of sixty dollars.*
Papers on this subject will be received, till the first day of January, 1798.

VI.

For the best experimental treatise on native American vegetable dies; accompanied with an accurate account of the vegetables employed——*A premium of ninety dollars.*
Papers on this subject will be received, till the first day of February, 1798.

VII.

For the best construction or improvement of lamps; especially, for lighting the streets ——*A premium of fifty dollars.*
Papers on this subject will be received, till the first day of April, 1797.

GENERAL CONDITIONS.

1. Every candidate, along with his performance, is to send to the society a sealed letter, containing his name and place of abode; which letter shall never be opened by the society, except in the case of a successful candidate.
2. No performance, invention or improvement, on any of the subjects proposed, for which a patent or any other reward shall have been obtained, before presenting it to the society, shall be considered as entitled to the premium.
3. In lieu of the money which shall be awarded by the society, as a premium, any successful candidate shall have it in his option to receive a gold or silver medal, or piece of plate, with a suitable inscription, of equal value.
4. The society reserve to themselves the power of giving, in all cases, such part only of any premium proposed, as the performance shall be adjudged to deserve; or, of withholding the whole, if it shall appear to have no merit above what may have been already published on the subject. The candidates may, however, be assured, that the society will always judge ... erally of their several claims.

This announcement from the American Philosophical Society describes the premiums, or prizes, for papers on a wide variety of "useful" subjects, including seventy dollars for "the best construction or improvement of ship-pumps," sixty dollars for "the best...improvement of stoves, or fire-places," sixty dollars for "the best method...of preventing the premature decay of Peach-trees," and ninety dollars for "the best experimental treatise on native American vegetable dies."

This engraving shows the meeting of a learned, or scientific, society in London. At this meeting, one scientist is demonstrating an electrical experiment for other members of the society.

ASTRONOMY

Astronomy, the study of the stars and planets, is one of the oldest "pure sciences." Many ancient civilizations developed sophisticated astronomical methods for predicting the movement of stars and planets. After the invention of the telescope in the seventeenth century, astronomy made tremendous progress; its chief practical use was in navigation and timekeeping.

Americans were interested in astronomy, as they were in all sciences. The earliest accomplished American astronomer was David Rittenhouse, who built the first telescope in America. In 1767, Rittenhouse also constructed the first accurate orrery, or model of the movements of the planets. Like those of many early American scientists, Rittenhouse's accomplishments are all the more impressive for the fact that he had almost no formal schooling.

This page of Latin text (right) is from a book by Johannes Kepler called Harmonies of the World, *published in 1619. In this section, Kepler, the brilliant German scientist, assigned musical values to the movement of the planets. Kepler's greatest achievement was the development of three laws that accurately described the motion of the planets around the sun.*

This engraving of David Rittenhouse (1732–86; opposite, top) was made after a painting by Charles Willson Peale. Rittenhouse began his distinguished scientific career as a maker of clocks and instruments, and later became a surveyor. As a surveyor, he helped to mark the boundaries between several states. Rittenhouse became the second president of the American Philosophical Society in 1791, after Benjamin Franklin's death.

The forty-foot reflecting telescope, built by Sir William Herschel (1738–1822), was the largest and most powerful telescope that had yet been built. Herschel's discovery of the planet Uranus in 1781 made him one of the most prominent astronomers of his day. In astronomy, as in all the sciences, the advances in the scientific community in Europe were closely followed in America. This engraving (below) of the telescope appeared in a magazine published in London.

THE INVENTIONS OF BENJAMIN FRANKLIN

Benjamin Franklin's theories and discoveries about electricity were some of the most exciting scientific advances made in early America. Although his achievements were built on the work of earlier experimenters, it was Franklin who sparked public interest in the subject. The most practical result of his experiments was the invention of the lightning rod, a simple but effective way of preventing fires caused by lightning.

Franklin's interests were extremely broad. Although he made his living as a printer and publisher, he was also an important American diplomat and one of the founders and the first president of the American Philosophical Society for Promoting Useful Knowledge. But it is for his inventions that Franklin is best remembered. In addition to the lightning rod, Franklin's inventions include the Franklin stove, which produced more heat than a regular fireplace could and burned less fuel, and bifocal eyeglasses.

Franklin was beloved both at home and abroad, where he was considered the personification of the new American spirit: energetic, bold, and ready to rise to the many different challenges of a new nation.

Benjamin Franklin's Experiments and Observations on Electricity *(right) was the most important scientific book published in early America. This title page is from the fifth edition of the book (a good indication of how popular it was). The book was published in London in 1774, twenty-three years after it was first published in America. It was Franklin who gave the electrical charges the names "positive" and "negative." His most important electrical theory is known as "the law of the conservation of charge."*

This print (opposite, bottom) shows the famous experiment in which Franklin flew a kite during a thunderstorm and proved that lightning was a form of electricity. The kite string was a wire, which ended in a key; when lightning struck the kite, it created a spark in the key. The experiment was extremely dangerous, and several scientists who later attempted to copy it were killed.

It was some time after the initial discovery of electricity before scientists learned how to harness the power to drive a machine. This engraving (below) from Pennsylvania Magazine *shows a "new electrical machine."*

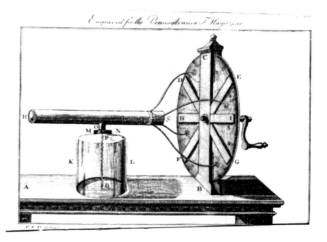

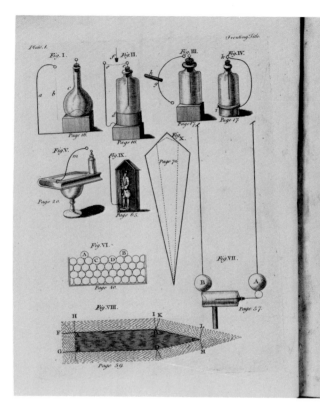

EXPERIMENTS
AND
OBSERVATIONS
ON
ELECTRICITY,
MADE AT
PHILADELPHIA in AMERICA,
BY
BENJAMIN FRANKLIN, L.L.D. and F.R.S.

Member of the Royal Academy of Sciences at Paris, of the Royal Society at Gottingen,
and of the Batavian Society in Holland, and President of the Philosophical Society
at Philadelphia.

To which are added,

LETTERS and PAPERS
ON
PHILOSOPHICAL SUBJECTS.

The Whole corrected, methodized, improved, and now collected into
one Volume, and illustrated with COPPER PLATES.

THE FIFTH EDITION.

LONDON:
Printed for F. NEWBERY, at the Corner of St. Paul's Church-Yard.
M.DCC.LXXIV.

INVENTIONS FOR AGRICULTURE

Agriculture was the first and by far the most important industry in early America. While farmers in the North continued to farm mainly to support themselves and their families and had little extra produce to sell, Southern farmers began to grow substantial cash crops like tobacco, cotton, rice, and sugar for export.

Technological improvements in agricultural methods were crucial to taming the wild land that the settlers found. While Europe had no shortage of agricultural labor, American farmers worked under very different conditions. America was short of labor for much of its early history, a condition that greatly spurred invention— although it also encouraged slavery. Machines that could increase a man or woman's productivity were sought after and eagerly experimented with.

The cotton gin (above), invented by Eli Whitney in 1793, was a simple but exceedingly important invention. Improved spinning technology made cotton a much more useful fiber, but extracting the seeds from each cotton ball by hand was so time-consuming that it slowed the development of a cotton industry. Whitney's invention pulled the cotton through a set of teeth, which caught and separated the seeds. The impact of the cotton gin was tremendous. It made cotton the basis of the Southern economy, which in turn reinforced the claim that slavery was an economic necessity. The conflict between the slave-based, agricultural economy in the South and an increasingly industrial economy in the North was a factor leading to the Civil War in 1861.

Christopher Tully offered an illustration (opposite, top) of his improved spinning wheel in Pennsylvania Magazine. *Spinning was done by hand with a spindle and distaff until the invention of the spinning wheel in the Middle Ages. Improvements in spinning technology helped spur a worldwide textile industry that was fed by cotton grown in the American South.*

This illustration (right) from Pennsylvania Magazine *shows an early threshing machine. Threshing machines, which separate grain from its stalk, were an improvement over manual threshing, in which the harvested stalks were beaten to separate the grain. The first simple threshing machines were put into use in America before the end of the eighteenth century.*

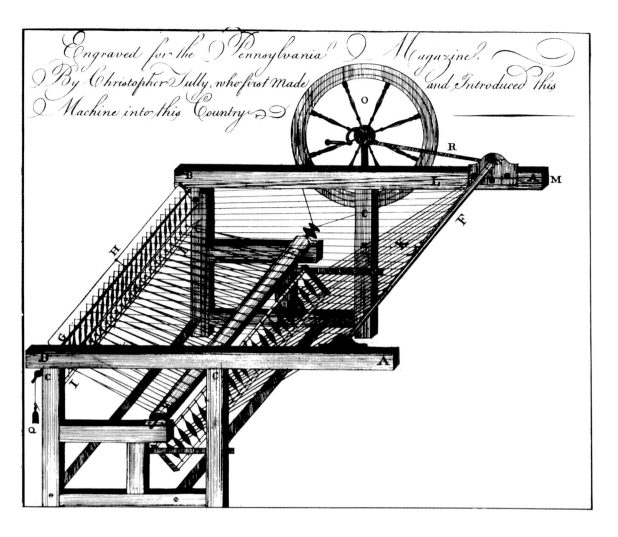

Engraved for the Pennsylvania Magazine. By Christopher Tully, who first Made and Introduced this Machine into this Country

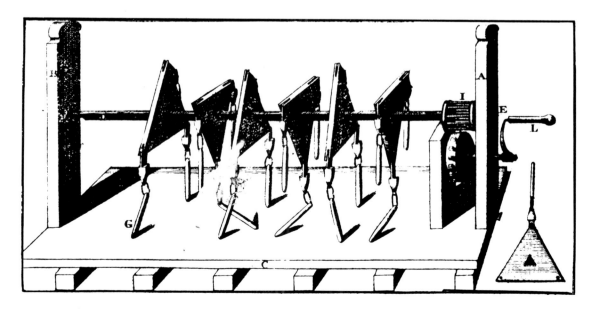

INVENTIONS IN TRANSPORTATION

Travel in early America was difficult and time-consuming. Roads were few, and most were little more than narrow trails open only to horseback riders, not to carts or carriages. Indians and dangerous animals made road travel even less appealing. Water was the preferred method of travel, but ships kept irregular schedules and at first were more likely to cross the Atlantic Ocean than sail up and down the American coast. Rivers were therefore the only practical means of traveling inland. Even so, America's unimproved waterways offered a difficult passage, and were open only to small boats.

Improvements in methods of transportation were vital to a growing American economy. Better transportation was not only important in opening the Western frontier but essential in getting the goods grown or made in one place to the rest of the nation or the world. Although early trails gradually developed into passable roads, development was expensive and slow. Most of the improvements in America's early transportation system had to do with water transport. They included development of ports and harbors that could accommodate large cargo ships and the creation of a network of navigable rivers by building canals and locks.

This machine for dredging harbors (top) was illustrated for Pennsylvania Magazine *in 1775. Early American settlements were made around natural harbors. But as the colonies prospered, larger and larger ships were required to transport goods to and from America, and many of these natural harbors were quickly outgrown. The invention of improved dredges, which dug channels into ports and harbors to give access to large ships, was an important step in the development of the American economy.*

John Fitch (1743–98) invented the first working steamboat in 1787. After the successful trial of a forty-five-foot boat on the Delaware River, Fitch built a larger steamboat, which carried passengers and cargo between Philadelphia and Burlington, New Jersey. Although Fitch's paddle-wheeled vessels provided reliable transportation, he was a poor businessman and never demonstrated that steam power could be profitable. This engraving (right) was made for Columbian Magazine, *which published Fitch's description of his steamboat in December 1786 and January 1787. It was not until Robert Fulton's* Clermont *traveled the Hudson River from New York to Albany in 1807 that the era of steamship travel really began. Steam-powered ships made a dramatic difference in the transportation of people and goods in America. Freed from the wind and tides, steamboats were able to make regularly scheduled trips up and down rivers and even back and forth across the Atlantic Ocean.*

Resource Guide

Key to picture positions: (T) top, (C) center, (B) bottom; and in combinations: (TL) top left, (TC) top center, (TR) top right, (BL) bottom left, (BC) bottom center, (BR) bottom right, (CR) center right, (CL) center left.

Key to picture locations within the Library of Congress collections (and where available,

photo-negative numbers): P - Prints and Photographs; HABS - Historical American Buildings Survey (div. of Prints and Photographs); R - Rare Book Division; G - General Collections; MSS - Manuscript Division; G&M - Geography and Map Division.

PICTURES IN THIS VOLUME

2-3 West Point, P, USZ62-40976 **4-5** bookplate, R **6-7** surgery, P

Timeline: **8** T, Columbus, G; CL, Pope Alexander, P, USZ62-49700; CR, totem, G **9** T, Shakespeare, G; CL, seal, R; CR, fort, P, USZ62-5139; BL, Smith, P; BR, Pocahontas, P, USZ62-39316 **10** T, fire, G; C, Locke, G; BL, title page, R; BR, Eliot, G **11** T, Louis XIV, G; C, Philip, P, USZ62-9234; B, college, P **12** TL, Marlborough, G; TR, seal, P, USZ62-676; C, cottage, P, USZ62-33762; B, mission, HABS **13** T, Swift, G; C, trial, G **14** TL, Frederick, G; TR, Rousseau, G; C, cartoon, P, USZ62-9701; B, title page, MSS **15** TL, Lavoisier, G; TR, Bastille, G; C, Adams, P, D416-509; B, steamboat, P, USZ62-1362

Part I: **16-17** Franklin, P, D416-311 **18-19** BL, tablet, G; TR, cave painting, P, USZ62-49642; BR, hieroglyphics, G **20-21** TL, Stuyvesant, P; BL, Indian, G; TR, Mather, G; BR, box painting, G **22-23** TL, Penn, P; TR, Mrs. West, P, D429-48142 **24-25** TL, Nebot, P, D416-438; BL, Greenleaf, P, D416-299; TR, Washington, P, D416-364 **26-27** TL, Adams, P, USZ62-5230; TR, Izzards, P, D416-203 **28-29** TL, Trumbull, P; TR, Hamilton, P, USZ62-6101A; BR, Indian, G **30-31** BL, Lexington, P, USZ62-13636; TR, Bouquet, P, USZ62-104; BR, Quebec, P, D416-701 **32-33** BL, Yorktown, P, D416-28047; TR, Washington, P, D416-9870; BR, Treaty, G **34-35** Shark, P, D429-48031 **36-37** BL, mountain pass, P, USZ62-46028; TR, Greenwoods, P, USZ62-45576; BR, Niagara Falls, P **38-39** TR, Philadelphia, P, USZ62-16615; BR, Boston, P, USZ62-45389 **40-41** TL, Venus, P, D429-48236; TR, Goddess, P, USZ62-15369 **42-43** BL, crucifixion, G; TR, skeleton, P, USZ62-60591; BR, tombstone, P, USZ62-52261 **44-45** TL, Washington, P, USZ62-7866; TR, Jones, P, USA7-24557; BR, George III, P, USZ62-22023 **46-47** TL, *Cato Major*, G; TR, *Bloody Arena*, G; C, *Pilgrim's Progress*, P, USZ62-58184; BR, Poems, P, USZ62-56850 **48-49** TL, *Day of Doom*, R; TC, Private Journal, R; TR, *Elegiac Sonnets*, G; BC, *Tenth Muse*, R; BR, America, P, USZ62-34154 **50-51** TL, Psalm Tunes, R; TR, Anacreontic, P, USZ62-44587 **52-53**

TL, A Song, MSS; TR, Yankee Doodle, P, USZ62-76203; BR, instrument makers, R **54-55** TL, Vaudevil, G; TC, *Henry IV*, R; TR, *Ponteach*, R; BR, theater, P, USZ62-64450 **56-57** TL, theater, P, USZ62-56353; BL, Constant Couple, G; BR, building, P, USZ62-1221 **58-59** TL, Penn house, G; BL, plan, G; BC, Revere house, P, USZ62-48899; TR, Mt. Pleasant, USZA1-224; BL, Mt. Airy, HABS **60-61** TL, stairs, P, USZ62-47408; TC, title page, P, USZ62-58164; BL, Carlyle, P, USZA1-418; TR, Mt. Vernon, HABS; BR, Tontine, P, USZ62-31136 **62-63** TL, King's, P, D4-71420; BL, St. Paul's, P, USZ62-31798; TR, Christ, HABS; BR, interior, P, USZ62-45711 **64-65** TL, Williamsburg, P, USZ62-2104; BL, Independence Hall, P, USZ62-17112; TR, Annapolis, P, USZ62-7974; BR, plan, P, USZ62-37227 **66-67** TL, Exchange, HABS; BL, Federal Hall, P, USZ62-45577; TR, convent, HABS; BR, mission, HABS

Part II: **68-69** experiment, P, USZ62-29022 **70-71** TL, title page, R; BL, bird, P, USZ62-358; TR, eagle, R; BR, snake, P, USZ62-00359 **72-73** TL, title page, R; BL, raccoon, R; TR, map, R; BR, herrings, P, USZ62-31148 **74-75** TL, title page, R; BL, flower, R; BC, tortoise, R; TR, Indian, P, USZ62-678; BR, list, MSS **76-77** TL, Mather, P, USZ62-22032; BL, title page, G; TR, Receipts, USZ62-74067 **78-79** TL, chart, P, USZ62-49991; TR, dentist, R; BR, surgery, R **80-81** TL, Cochrane, G; TR, plan, G; C, hospital, G; BR, surgery kit, G **82-83** TL, Rush, P, USZ62-28646; BL, seal, P; TR, Pennsylvania Hospital, P, USZ62-56359; BR, Massachusetts Hospital, HABS **84-85** TL, vessels, P, USZ62-31810; BL, laboratory, P, USZ62-29044; TR, Premiums, MSS; BR, meeting, P, USZ62-29045 **86-87** TL, Rittenhouse, P, USZ62-26481; BL, Harmonies, P, USZ62-95170; TR, telescope, P, USZ62-33497 **88-89** BL, electrical machine, P, USZ62-55059; TR, title page, P, USZ62-95337; BR, lightning, P, USZ62-1433 **90-91** TL, cotton gin, P, USZ62-37202; TR, spinning wheel, P, USZ62-37785; BR, threshing machine, P, USZ62-55060 **92-93** TC, dredge, P, USZ62-31146; BR, steam boat, P, USZ62-31148

SUGGESTED READING

DANIEL, CLIFTON. *Chronicle of America*. New York: Prentice Hall, 1989.
DONOVAN, FRANK R. *The Many Worlds of Benjamin Franklin*. Mahwah, N.J.: Troll Associates, 1963.
FLEXNER, THOMAS J. *America's Old Masters*. New York: Dover, 1967.

HORNUNG, CLARENCE P. *Treasury of American Design and Antiques*. New York: Abrams, 1976.
MOSCOW, HENRY. *Thomas Jefferson and His World*. Mahwah, N.J.: Troll Associates, 1963.
READER'S DIGEST. *America's Historic Places: An Illustrated Guide to Our Country's Past*. New York: Reader's Digest, 1988.

Index

Page numbers in *italics* indicate illustrations.